LIFE

THE ULTIMATE VIDEO GAME

An Inspiration Manual to
Level Up Your Life

KING KANYINI

TABLE OF CONTENTS

QUICK START GUIDE

Life is just like a video game.

This revelation came to me on a crisp afternoon at a go-kart track in Salt Lake City, while I was chatting with a good friend of mine. We were there during our annual snowboarding trip with his kids, and I found myself reflecting on how life presents us with opportunities for growth - what most call "problems" - and how these challenges provide the necessary experience points to level up and reach our highest potential.

Minutes later, my friend would face one of these “opportunities of growth” when another go-kart driver cut him off, triggering a cascade of anger that nearly got him ejected from the track. As he confronted both the driver and an official who hadn't even witnessed the incident, I gently touched his shoulder and whispered into his ear, "If life is a video game uhhhh, you are FAILING this level."

He paused, looked at me, laughed and said, "You know what, you're right."

I then saw him choose a different path, and instead of berating the hapless teenager, he apologized to the young official and walked back to his family. After the moment passed, my creative wheels started spinning.

What if life WAS just like a video game? What if we had all of the tools and skills within us to accomplish our wildest dreams, but we just forgot them? Just imagine...

We spend our early years learning by experience, absorbing the world around us through the lens of wonder and possibility. Our imagination runs wild, and everything feels new and full of potential - until it isn't. Until the day that pain, loss, and suffering enters our story, and we begin building walls to keep ourselves safe. It's on that infamous day that we lose a crucial part of ourselves, our inner child. But worry not, because I'm here to help you get them back.

What you hold in your hands is more than just a book - it's a key to reconnect with that child who dreamed without limits, that saw the Universe as an infinite playground of possibilities. Where did that inner child go? Perhaps you catch glimpses of them in the young ones around you - your children, nieces, or nephews - but these are just reflections of who you once were. Reflections of who you can be again.

Life: The Ultimate Video Game transforms life's challenges and traumas into engaging levels waiting to be conquered. Through ancient wisdom reframed through the lens of gaming - breathwork, visualization, meditation, biohacking and more - you'll activate the tools to clear stages in life you've been stuck in, and finally collect the precious wisdom they hold. Even better, you'll have fun doing it! Because who said that self-transformation had to be difficult and boring?

The cherry on top of this transformational cake is that something even more profound is waiting for you beyond the healing. As you progress through this inspiration manual, you're embarking on a quest to recover something irreplaceable. Somewhere in a distant castle, a part of you is waiting - waiting to be rescued. You may have hid them away to protect them from experiencing more pain, loss, and suffering. But the truth is, though they may be sheltered from suffering, YOU still carry that weight. This book will, level by level, arm you with the skills and abilities needed to finally bring that part of you home. So you can finally be reunited with your inner child, and remember this truth:

Life isn't happening TO you,
Life is happening FOR you,
to learn from, and level up.

I know this path intimately because I've walked every step of it. From a humble home in Spokane, WA, where video games became my safe space through death, divorce, and poverty, to the halls of Princeton as a mechanical engineer, and into a successful but stressful finance job in Manhattan - games were my constant companion, my teacher, my sanctuary.

Then one day, everything changed. COVID hit, and I found myself in the epicenter of the pandemic, riding my bike down an eerily empty 5th avenue past the Metropolitan Museum on a surreal Sunday afternoon. While many people turned to video games during the lockdown, I discovered something far more powerful - my purpose in helping people heal from their traumas.

My journey of transformation took me from Chris Benson, the successful ivy-league finance bro, to receiving the name Kanyini, which means "in each other, we find ourselves." And it was in the heart of this tragic event where millions of lives were being lost, that I found myself.

As a healing practitioner, a 2nd degree reiki healer, breathmaster, AADP health coach, and modern shaman, I've spent 10 years intensely studying the healing arts. Currently pursuing a doctorate in integrative medicine, I hold space with my wife Zai'Ra at our healing retreat, Amaroo Sanctuary, where we've witnessed countless miracles of transformation. From these experiences, I have channeled and distilled this book.

The path ahead will revolutionize how you experience life's challenges and opportunities. You'll learn to see obstacles as opportunities to earn experience points, trauma as treasure chests of wisdom waiting to be unlocked, and your own consciousness as the most powerful gaming console ever played.

Through each chapter, or level, you'll master practical tools that enhance your real-world abilities, collect Gems of Understanding from every experience, and develop authentic spiritual connections through consistent practice.

The most beautiful part? All you need to do is read, complete the missions, and approach each challenge with an open heart and willing mind. This isn't like any book you've ever read. It's a bridge between the worlds of gaming and healing, between who you are and who you're meant to become, all through an epic adventure. Essentially, it's an immersive video game, in book form. And what would a gamified book be, without a companion app?

Yup, **Life: The Ultimate Video Game (LTUVG) App** is a fully functional companion app with missions, tools, resources, and the best part? Cutscenes. Because what is an experiential video game without some engaging cutscenes?

Why are cutscenes important? Well besides being dope, a picture says a thousand words, and we're going to be introducing some cutting edge concepts that I want you to absorb easier and faster!

So throughout every level of this book, you'll find missions that you will progress through simultaneously with the app.

The flow will work like this: Each level will introduce a concept, which will be broken up into different missions. After you are introduced to that particular mission, you will be prompted to log into the LTUVG App, navigate to that particular mission and follow the guided videos/cutscenes.

After each mission, there will be a mission log, or journal entry, that will be required in order to unlock the next content. Then you will return to the book for the next mission, most likely the following day (we want to pace out your progress, no binging).

And if you need more direction, there is an entire animated video in the app dedicated to walking you through the process.

Don't worry, the app is simple to use, fun, and engaging. My goal is to get you wins early and often with this book, so you'll keep coming back to level up your life.

So, are you ready to press start on the greatest adventure of all? The journey back to yourself?

Great, but first, let's make sure you are fully prepared for this quest.

PROLOGUE

PREPARING FOR YOUR ADVENTURE

Every great adventure begins with a moment of preparation, a sacred pause before stepping through the threshold of transformation. Before we embark on this journey together, there are three essential elements to gather, like collecting the mythic items needed before a legendary quest:

Your first item, or reward, is the LTUVG app - a digital companion that holds the keys to your transformation. Within it lies a repository of missions, meditations, cutscenes, and most importantly, a thriving community of fellow adventurers walking this path alongside you. Scan the QR code below (or go to www.ltuvg.com) and enter the password LEVELUPMYLIFE to unlock 90 days of full access to our growing fellowship. After the 3 month trial, all missions and exercises remain eternally yours, supporting your continued evolution, but continued community access is $5.55 per month, less than a cup of coffee.

Next, you'll need your mission log, aka journal. I personally have a journal from Barnes and Noble that I love, but I also use the *Day One* app if you prefer a digital journal to take on the go. This will become your personal chronicle, recording the Gems of Understanding you discover along the way, the breakthroughs that reshape your reality, and the transformation that unfolds within you.

Journaling is crucial for leveling up faster because of a concept called "multi-sensory learning." This approach is based on the science that the brain processes information better when multiple pathways are activated simultaneously. This helps you create stronger neural connections and improve your ability to recall and apply knowledge.

So, when you journal your experience, you are one, writing it down, two, recalling it as you write, and three, crystalizing the memory so you can read it out loud to yourself later. Think of this as an XP multiplier for our leveling up process, and who doesn't want those XP multipliers while gaming?

Finally, and perhaps most crucially, **take a moment to set your intention**.

Let yourself dream deeply of what "leveling up your life" means to you. And dream big. Is it: finding work-life balance, creating financial freedom, finding your purpose and a fulfilling career, meeting the person of your dreams? Whatever will create your dream life - write it down.

Let it become both your North Star and your foundation as we begin this extraordinary journey together.

THE JOURNEY AHEAD

YOUR PATH TO TRANSFORMATION

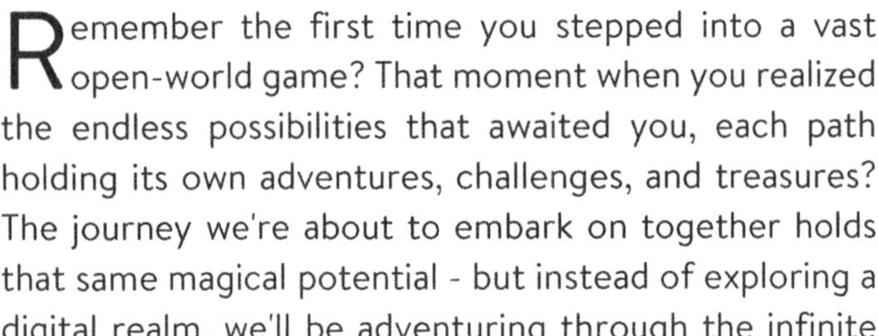

Remember the first time you stepped into a vast open-world game? That moment when you realized the endless possibilities that awaited you, each path holding its own adventures, challenges, and treasures? The journey we're about to embark on together holds that same magical potential - but instead of exploring a digital realm, we'll be adventuring through the infinite landscape of your own consciousness.

This inspiration manual unfolds across fourteen transformative levels, each one carefully designed to awaken dormant abilities within you while utilizing your gaming experience to reinforce these concepts. As a man of science, I also will be weaving in scientific support for every concept from peer reviews and evidence-based science, to cutting edge quantum physics theories.

But the biggest thing that will get you through this book? Curiosity. As I ask often, suspend disbelief, and keep an open mind on what you are about to experience, follow your excitement, trust your heart, and I will walk you through the extraordinary adventure that awaits you:

We begin exactly where every great RPG starts, by pulling you into the center of the story. Level 1 takes you through your own character creation sequence, utilizing your real life characteristics to manifest your own Spirit Avatar, with a twist. Just as every character in games like Final Fantasy or Elder Scrolls begin with natural affinities, you too have unique attributes waiting to be fully activated.

Once you see yourself in the Game of Life, we'll then equip you with your first skill, coherent breathing, and empower you with the science behind why it's the single most thing you can do to tap into your natural gifts AND improve your quality of health by up to 40-50%!

Using breathwork as a gateway, Level 2 opens the door to what I call the subtle energy realm. You will be introduced to the main skill trees that you will be leveling up to start the book. This is what I call your V.I.S.A., or your passport into this energetic realm. A realm of unlimited possibilities. Together, we'll learn fun new methods to increase our ability to be vulnerable, to activate our intuition, to expand upon serving others, and to magnify our awareness of the energetic world around us.

Think of it like discovering you're not just a warrior with a sword, but a battlemage who can also wield ancient magic. These aren't just stats on a character sheet;

they're your authentic superpowers that have been dormant, waiting for the right moment to awaken. That moment is now. We'll close out this level with our first boss battle. Where you will use all of the skills and abilities learned thus far to transform your deepest pain, into your greatest power, through forgiveness.

In Level 3, you'll discover something mind-bending - your YOUniverse. Did you know that ancient civilizations believe that, just like an MMORPG, we aren't 8 billion people in one world, but 8 billion worlds sharing one collective consciousness?[1] Here you'll learn about the quantum science behind the origin of our bodies of consciousness, and how we can utilize our imagination to connect with the planet, and the infinite wisdom that exists within our DNA.

After an intense first three levels where we upgrade the crap out of you, Level 4 takes a bit of a break for a love story. A love story about myself and Zai'Ra, the love of my lifetimes. I'll share an epic ballad about falling in love, miraculous healing, and a journey into Mordor. Yes, we lived our own version of *The Fellowship of the Ring* and survived. On brand with this chapter, you'll also learn some ancient cleansing techniques that will be invaluable to you as you level up your life. Just as you'd never face a boss battle without the right equipment, these ancient techniques prepare you for the journey ahead.

Level 5 is where the world really opens up. While your V.I.S.A. is your passport to the subtle energy realm, the 6Cs of Universal Principles are the skill trees that will allow you to thrive in this amazing world. Think of them as the physics engine running your reality - once you understand how they work, you can begin to play the game in an entirely new level of awareness. This isn't about exploiting glitches; it's about aligning yourself with the fundamental forces that shape existence.

I can't wait for you to get to this level, because then I get to teach you a new way to meditate. One that, even in this fast paced world, will work for you. Because meditation is all about being present, not attempting to clear your mind of thoughts!

By Level 6, you'll understand why button-mashing never beats consistent, intentional, inspired action. This is why legends like Michael Jordan, Kobe Bryant, and Lebron James were unbeatable. It is because no one worked more consistently than they did. Don't worry, you don't have to be like Mike to win in life. Because in this level, I will give you some amazing life hacks so that you can build sustainable practices that compound your growth over time. Just imagine, if you become 1% better every day at one thing, after just one year of daily improvement, you will be 37 times better at that thing!

Remember grinding for experience points or materials in your favorite RPG? Life works the same way - and I'll show you how to make the grinding both efficient and enjoyable with some engaging immersive and life upgrading activities. As I said, I'm all about getting you consistent and easy wins.

Level 7 unlocks what might be the most powerful ability in the game - compassion. Not the surface-level kind, but the deep, transformative force that enhances every other skill you possess. This is also a key to getting back on the consistency wagon when we inevitably fall off. The science on this is surprising, but it's actually compassion that encourages us to maintain new habits instead of beating ourselves up about it. Do you see how these chapters are starting to build on one another like a nicely designed video game? Let's keep going.

In Level 8, we learn to lean into our creativity to overcome life's challenges with compassion. Through specially designed missions, you'll reconnect with this superpower that makes life truly extraordinary. Like a master builder in the Lego Movie, I'll teach you how to activate "creative mode" in Minecraft, except this will be activated in your real life. It's at this point you'll begin to truly see and feel the imagination revolution that this book is igniting. Because the key to the greatest gaming system we have is our imagination.

But to understand the profound extent of your imagination, we introduce clarity as the next Universal Principle in Level 9. This level isn't just about mental clarity; it's also about the epiphanies that emerge when you're able to see the bigger picture of why your life IS, your life. Like reaching that moment in Final Fantasy when the true nature of your journey becomes clear, this level reveals the deeper purpose behind every challenge you've faced. Here you'll learn to weave together all your awakening abilities into a questline of understanding that illuminates the path ahead.

By the end of this level, you will be ready for your second big boss challenge, where we tap into the energetic wisdom within your body to upgrade your seven energy centers in the Trials of the Sacred Chakras.

Level 10 is your bonus level! Your reward for all the consistency and courage you've embodied. This is where you'll be rewarded with your very own Spirit Animal! Your companion that will assist you in overcoming life's biggest challenges. Which means, that from this level on, we are approaching the summit of the castle holding your inner child.

Just as we must face increasingly difficult levels in games to grow stronger, this stage teaches you to transmute your fear into resolve, your anxiety into acceptance. Because the truth is, every legendary quest requires us to step beyond our comfort zone to earn what matters most.

Level 11 forges your courage into conviction. I start the book asking you to "suspend your disbelief" to create space for magic to happen. This level is a reminder that while our imagination is our superpower; our greatest limitations are our expectations. It is through your own experience throughout LTUVG, that we are building an unshakeable faith not just in yourself, but in the entire remembrance of your consciousness. It is in this final remembrance that you earn your final summons, your Divine Guardian Counsel. This is your final supporting cast that you can use to help fulfill your ultimate goal. That is the goal you set when you started this book -to retrieve your inner child.

Level 12 is where everything comes together - where all your tools, abilities, and understanding merge into a symphony of mastery. Like finally understanding how to chain all your abilities together in a powerful RPG, you'll see how each skill you've gained serves a greater purpose. This is where you prepare for what awaits in that far off castle - the reunion with your inner child.

Level 13 presents the epic conclusion of this arc of your journey. Here you'll use everything you've learned, every tool you've mastered, every Gem of Understanding you've collected, every guide you can summon, to finally reach that distant castle where your inner child awaits. Just as every great game builds toward a meaningful culmination, every skill and insight you've gained has prepared you for this profound moment of reunion.

Level 14 is pure celebration and jubilation! Here I share one more miraculous healing, a western medical miracle, that is a result of the inner child reunion my beloved Zai'Ra experienced. I share this final inspirational story to remind you that this isn't the end of your journey; it's the beginning of a whole new way of living life to its fullest potential. Like discovering a New Game+ mode, but in real life - where everything you've learned takes on deeper meaning and application.

Again, your trusty companion in this journey is the LTUVG app - more than just a digital guide, it's your gateway to a thriving community of fellow adventurers. Each mission you complete earns you badges that mark your progress and contribute to your position on the community leaderboard. But this isn't about competition - it's about celebration and mutual support on this path of transformation.

Within the app you'll find:

- Interactive missions that bring each level to life
- A vibrant community sharing their own journeys
- Gamification features to keep things fun and exciting including dope achievement badges, monthly leaderboards, and in-game currency to purchase future DLC (downloadable content).
- Special video content that deepens your understanding.
- World challenges that help you maintain momentum and solidify concepts.

Remember, this isn't just another self-help journey - it's a sacred quest to recover the most precious parts of yourself. Every mission you complete, every badge you earn, every connection you make in the community brings you closer to that moment of reunion with your inner child - the part of you that never forgot how to see the magic in everyday life.

I've walked this path myself, transforming from a finance professional trapped in survival mode to someone who witnesses and facilitates miracles of healing. These aren't just theories or pleasant ideas - they're battle-tested techniques that have helped countless others rediscover their own magic and retrieve an invaluable part of yourself.

To truly experience the transformation this book offers, you must commit to both reading and doing. The recommended pace to complete the book is one to two missions per day. Listen to your body and pace yourself so that you are fully integrating these new skills into your life.

As I said, this is more than just a book - it's a portal to remembering who you truly are; where every challenge becomes an opportunity for growth, every setback a setup for a comeback, and every moment a chance to collect the experience points needed to finally bring your inner child home.

I would like to give you context of the type of experience this book will provide you. One of my many clients shared this after a successful reunion, “I didn’t come out of this experience a different person, I came out my full self... you can’t put a price on that.”

So, are you ready to embark on the greatest rescue mission of all time? To step into your power as both the player and the hero of your own story? To finally know who you truly are and remember your own magic?

Then let's begin. Your destiny - and your inner child - await.

Disclaimer: *While breathwork is 100% safe, if you have a history of epilepsy, glaucoma, cardiovascular disease, severe mental illness, osteoporosis, aneurysms, strokes, seizures or neurological conditions, or are in your third trimester of pregnancy, please consult with a doctor before doing any of the intense breathwork in this book.*

LEVEL 0

INTRODUCING LIFE: THE ULTIMATE VIDEO GAME

Life: The Ultimate Video Game, what in the world does that mean?

It's exciting, intriguing, unbelievable, and yet it is the title of this book that inspired you to open in. Have you ever felt that life emulated a video game? Do you wish that life had its own instruction manual, so you didn't have to guess your way through life?

If you read the *Quick Start Guide*, you'll have heard the story of when I had this exact realization. I saw the parallels between my favorite role-playing games and how I have navigated my own life. In fact, I noticed how most of us might navigate life. And so I present to you the Inspiration Manual on how to play this game, called Life.

If you haven't read the *Quick Start Guide*, and are new this world, I highly recommend reading it. It will help prepare you for this epic-journey so you don't miss out on crucial tips, tricks, and experience points later on. Thank you for your trust and cooperation in advance.

I, like many of you, grew up when analog gaming was still a thing. When not having a cell phone was acceptable, and using MapQuest was the best way to go to a new friend's home. Nowadays, it isn't acceptable to be away from your phone for more than a day, for fear of someone getting upset that you didn't return their text. I have had the gift of opening up a regular Nintendo for Christmas, and the joy of being at home with our very first Macintosh computer! I fell in love with the digital age; I fell in with video games. As technology progressed and the dream of playing a lifelike video game became a real possibility, I couldn't wait to buy the newest system that came out; fantasizing about how good the new graphics would be.

Fast forwarding to the present day, you might expect that I would own the PS5 and Xbox One. Surprisingly, I own neither. My time gaming has been relegated to periodic moments of *Magic the Gathering Arena* on my phone in between client trips or breaks in writing, speaking engagements, and building healing communities in New York, Atlanta and Ecuador with my wife. By the time this book comes out I might also be DJing with a friend who is touring the world, who knows? The reason I don't own a video game system isn't because life has gotten too busy, it's because life has become my favorite video game to play.

I've learned how to transfer the thousands of hours I've spent gaming into real life experience points to create the life of my dreams. Even better, I am here now to show you how to do the same thing! Turning your gaming skills into real life abilities to level up your own life. The added bonus—this process will also reduce your stress, improve your focus, break bad habits, and increase your energy. It's a win-win situation. Life will feel as addictive as gaming is, and you'll live a healthier, fuller life!

If you are a fan of role-playing games or games with RPG features in them, perhaps you've already had this thought about life being like a video game. I started seeing synchronicities in life that did not happen by accident. Just like we have attributes in games, we have attributes in life. And no, not just the ones that we're used to being in games (strength, dexterity, etc.), but invisible attributes like intuition, awareness, and more; that can be honed and improved upon. Matter of fact, when I honed and improved upon these skills, it unlocked more tools and levels in life for me to overcome! I even unlocked some summons!

But before I get to that part of the book, you must be wondering, how did this realization occur? As many epic adventures begin, it started with a tragedy, COVID-19. My wife and I lived in New York City, an epicenter of the pandemic, and as the world shut down, a portal opened.

My heart goes out to all those who were affected by the pandemic with loss and hardship. At the same time, I truly believe that this was the hard reset that we as humanity needed to unplug from the distractions in life. Zai'Ra and I, like many around the world, also used this opportunity to plug into a deeper part of ourselves. A part that had been desperately waiting to wake up.

When we did, the Universe took us on an incredible journey. A journey to rescue our inner child that had been kidnapped by the traumas of our tumultuous lives. For my *Lord of the Rings* fans, we took a real-life journey to Mordor and lived to tell the tale. This book is a testament to the lessons learned, and I am grateful to share this wisdom with you so that you too, can level up your life, as if it were a video game. The skills that awaken within you will take you on an epic journey of transformative healing. A journey to rescue your own inner child so you can activate your superpowers from within.

Through my own deep loss, I've found that there were always "gems of understanding" that I gained on the other side of the pain. These gems are special "aha" moments where I gained a deeper understanding of why trauma served to awaken a part of the best possible version of myself. It is through this awakening that I've learned that we can transmute challenging moments into experiences of peace, triumph, and bliss.

For me, one gem of understanding, or GOU, from tragic loss was that my family lives on in my heart always, even after they transitioned from the physical realm. Thus, the more authentically I live from the heart, the more present I can be with my loved ones, whether they are alive or have passed on.

This book will help you accept and reframe past and present pain, so you can transmute it into "Gems of Understanding" or GOUs, as I will refer to them. Each GOU you gain will increase your ability to navigate life with the awareness that:

Life Doesn't Happen to You,
It Happens for You, To Level Up

By the end of this book, you will be a GOU ninja, earning exponential experience points (XP) from daily challenges that used to frustrate and drain your energy.

By the end of this book, when a tough challenge comes up, you will use your toolbox of new skills to transmute chaotic energy into organized flowing energy. You will be the hero in your own video game. Life will be exciting rather than excruciating.

By the end of this book, your friends, family, and even kids will love this version of you that is being reborn. A more playful version of yourself that can accomplish more, manifest more, stress less, and be more present in every moment of the day.

If you are thinking that this book is an easy button to level up without putting in necessary "life-gaming" hours, then maybe this book isn't for you. But if you are willing to have fun and put in the hours to learn some new skills, then this book is for you.

But fair warning, this is not a game genie, or a cheat code, to avoid the growth process. It will, however, simplify your growth process and shift the context for how you engage with the problems in your life, so these new skills FEEL like a cheat code.

You still must show up and do the work. But this "work" is designed to be fun, because we are on a journey to rescue our inner child, who remembers how to play. Our adult self has been told we cannot play anymore. That's why we love video games, because they allow us to play again. Through the levels and multimedia missions offered in the companion app, this interactive book will make life more enjoyable. But....

***I can't earn the experience points for you,
I can ONLY show you how to earn 100 percent of the experience points available to you.***

When life gets hard, think of it as a challenging level in a video game. Are you going to allow the levels in your life to defeat you and let hope be lost? I don't think you will, because you are here, and this game of life is designed for all of us to succeed, including you. We just forgot how to play the game.

It isn't your fault you forgot, it's nobody's fault, but it IS our responsibility to wake up! It is our responsibility to see that each challenge in life is a reminder of our strength and surrender, to what we can persevere through. Just like the video games you've conquered, Life The Ultimate Video Game (LTUVG) will empower you to live healthier, with more control over your emotions, a heightened sense of awareness, an innate ability to manifest whatever you want, and a strong desire to serve others from your heart in the process. You will feel lighter and happier. Your health and longevity will improve immensely, and life will become more fun and carefree!

Do you want this life? If you do, grab your journal -aka mission log- right now, open to the first page, and write down the date you started this book and underline it. Write:

"I commit to myself, to invest fifteen minutes a day,
sometimes more, to level up my life.
Every time I read LTUVG, I get 1 percent better at life.
Every level I complete in this manual will help me learn
something new about myself.
I love my life!"

After that, journal three to five minutes on your favorite video game or movie experience as a kid and how it made you feel. When you finish, if you haven't done this yet, download the LTUVG app, and join the Life Gamer Guild (LGG) in the Communities section. Find the "Proving Grounds Q&A" Channel, introduce yourself, name, location, what your favorite game/movie is and "I commit to having fun!"

Here is the QR Code for the app (or you can go to www.ltuvg.com) and use the code: LEVELUPMYLIFE to sign up for free. You will have lifetime full access to the content, and 3 months free trial to the community features, which is less than a cup of coffee ($5.55) per month to maintain access to that content.

Dive into the app and explore, it will activate this book like no other reading experience you've ever had. Make sure to watch the *welcome video*, it will excite you even more about this immersive reading experience and provide crucial information for you. It's your hub to access new missions as you progress through this manuscript to the Game of Life. As you complete quests, earn experience points, collect all the rewards and badges, and level up with like-minded adventurers, you will discover your new powers collectively. So be sure to look out for World Events and interact with one another to climb up the leaderboard and collect Life Quester coins, in-game currency you can use to upgrade your experience and show your mastery in the Game of Life.

And don't worry, you can complete this book without spending another penny, Life Quester Coins are simply your reward for staying active in the community and helping other Life Gamers level up. My version of karma for being a good Samaritan gamer.

Back to your commitment... why 1 percent better every day?

Remember the daily login bonuses in your favorite MMORPG (mass multiplayer online role-playing game)? Games like World of Warcraft, Final Fantasy XIV or any gacha game that reward you for simply showing up each day with extra gold, experience points, or special items? Now, imagine applying that same dedication to real life. Studies show that getting better bit by bit is more efficient than doing it in large chunks.

By committing just 5-15 minutes a day to 'Life Gaming' - improving yourself by 1 percent - you're claiming a daily login bonus for life. These small improvements compound dramatically over time. After one year of consistent 'logins', you'll have earned 37 times more experience points than when you started. Keep that streak going for two years? You'll have amassed an astounding 1400 times more XP!

As avid gamers, we often spend hours optimizing our characters for mere fractions of a percentage point improvement. Simply by reading this inspiration manual daily, you'll be adding a 37x multiplier to your XP earned in just one year!

And here's the kicker - this bonus XP doesn't even account for how much better you'll become at spotting and capitalizing on XP opportunities you previously missed. As you level up your awareness and skills, you'll start noticing XP all around you, in situations where you once saw none. It's like unlocking a secret XP multiplier that makes every interaction and experience more valuable.

Think about how much further along in life you'd be with that kind of growth. While others are stuck grinding the same levels, you'll be tackling challenges they can't even see yet. This isn't about getting ahead at others' expense - it's about unlocking your own potential to better serve and inspire those around you. You'll have the edge to not only improve your own life but to lift others up as well.

This compounding growth IS your cheat code for transforming life into the ultimate video game, where each day offers a new chance to claim your bonus and level up your real-world character.

The purpose of this book is to remind you of your favorite video games, and to teach that life, EVERY aspect of life, has an analogy and connection to a video game. As I share analogies to games that I love, I encourage you to use your own creativity to make your own connections with gaming and aspects of life. This is important, because that is what makes it real for you. My stories are only meant to serve as a mirror to help activate your own memories.

No two people are the same, and the analogies that will anchor your new skills may be different than mine. If that happens, please keep making that gaming connection within you, so that you will transfer this gaming skill into real life. Get excited about this journey!

We are about to show that anyone who's ever said "gaming is a waste of time" was sadly mistaken.

I'm also going to show you the controls, the mechanisms, the jump, crouch, and fly commands that allow you to control your worlds and let go of feeling like you need to control everything around you. Remember that famous saying?

"...Grant me the serenity to accept
the things I cannot change,
The courage to change the things I can,
And the wisdom to know the difference."

This inspiration manual will grant you these powers if you suspend disbelief long enough to let them seep in. The framework that will help you activate these abilities will be your imagination, or what I call your "Imagination Realization Station".

This is your revolutionary gaming console for this experience, and powering up this system is as easy as breathing. Literally. This is your first focus, because it's something you do every day, and it allows you to control your emotions, and thus, your experience.

Your breath is also the foundation for activating the power of your imagination and inner knowing with meditation, visualization, and biohacking. These practices have all been proven to immensely improve your quality of life. In addition, we will utilize our Imagination Realization Station (IR Station) to reframe aspects of life, like vulnerability and intuition, into individual attributes with skill trees that you can level up to level up your spirit avatar in life.

To create this avatar of yours, you will take a Unique & Universal Attribute Assessment Quiz, to see what archetype you are in LTUVG. We'll then explain the different bodies (or levels) of consciousness that exist within you, and how they all interact with your Universe. Next, we'll introduce the 6Cs of Universal Principles that each of our Universes are ruled by, how we can level up these individual skill trees and how they benefit our Universal attributes.

Before you ask what all of these new terms mean, be patient, stay the course, and it will become clear. Like any good video game, we will take it step by step, so that you feel confident with each new skill unlocked, to nurture your leveling up process. There will be online videos, guided journeys, and interactive produced media designed to make this reprogramming process fun and engaging. At the end of the day, this is a new type of game. Not augmented reality, but IR, Imagination Realization. Using our imagination to create our reality.

I say *reprogramming* because many of us already think we know how to play the game of life, because we are already living in it! Many reading this book have gotten pretty good at the game, whether you think of it as a game or not. And most of us, I would guess, have gotten to where we are in life, due to our Unique Attributes. These are our go-to abilities that we will cover, in the next chapter, or level, of this gamified book.

LEVEL 1

IDENTIFYING YOURSELF IN THE GAME

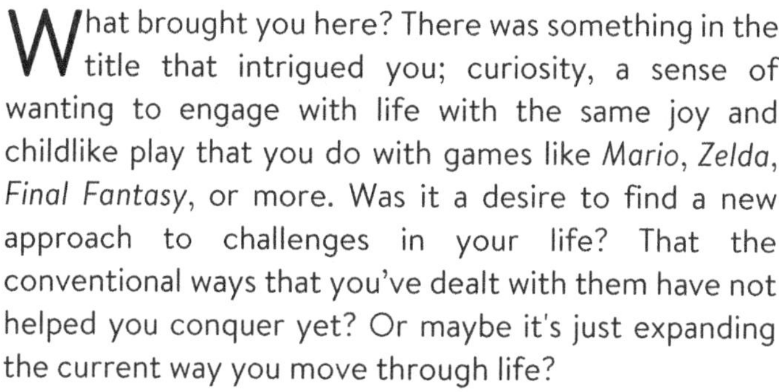

What brought you here? There was something in the title that intrigued you; curiosity, a sense of wanting to engage with life with the same joy and childlike play that you do with games like *Mario*, *Zelda*, *Final Fantasy*, or more. Was it a desire to find a new approach to challenges in your life? That the conventional ways that you've dealt with them have not helped you conquer yet? Or maybe it's just expanding the current way you move through life?

This inspiration manual for life is a proposal to bring fun into the process of overcoming life's challenges, while also creating the opportunity to finally break the chain of the trauma holding you back from your own superpowers. What are the things that might be holding you back?

This book will help if you are looking to relieve chronic stress, anxiety, or break bad habits, if you are looking to discover and/or supercharge your purpose in life, if you have an overcontrolling nature—a natural fear of uncertainty, or a fear of anything for that matter. If there is a lack of love, vulnerability, or motivation to connect with others, this manual will massively unlock your life. This manuscript will help anyone who can connect with the joy of gaming, to help them overcome life's challenges with a sense of fun and ease.

The first secret in learning how to engage with life as if it were a video game is to say, "My circumstances may not be my fault, but they are my responsibility." As I mentioned previously, this is because it's nobody's fault. We live in a society where blame and guilt are passed around like a hot potato. This is a distraction.

Imagine dying in a video game and writing to the developer to tell them it's their fault you died because the game was too difficult. If you've played Dark Souls, you might have considered this. I know I did.

But most people, including me, enjoy these challenging games because the reward of overcoming these difficulties is worth the journey. In life, it can be the same.

Will Smith shared a quote that really struck me, no pun intended, about fault vs responsibility.

"It may not be your fault you are in the situation you are in,
But it is your responsibility to figure out how to fix it… Especially when it involves your heart."

It is your responsibility to use your abilities to find a way through the maze of life that brings both intense pain and indescribable joy. Responsibility is not an admission of guilt; responsibility simply is the ability to respond. How do we start to improve our ability to respond to the challenges in life?

How would you respond to challenges in a video game? If this is *Final Fantasy*, *Elder Scrolls*, or *Zelda*, you would tap into an ability that was a tailored strength to overcome that challenge. Maybe if you were a mage (wizard) you would utilize a chain lightning spell to take out a mob of baddies. If you were a dual wielding rogue, utilize your dexterity to flow through the defenses of your enemies and strike them in the heart.

In the following exercise, we assess what we will refer to as your Unique Attributes, so that we can get a baseline of race, class, and skill set in the game of life. Then we will empower you with a toolkit of knowledge and skills so you can respond to any situation, utilizing a framework that you've developed as a kid playing video games!

Through consistent practice, we will build our imagination so that our creativity reframes daily challenges into daily missions through a "gaming" lens. This reframing will provide clarity in goals so that you can courageously and compassionately respond to each challenge. As you respond to these challenges with more presence, you will feel yourself gaining more XP and eventually having "aha" moments when you acquire GOUs.

This growth builds confidence, conviction and abilities. As daily missions get more difficult and challenging in different ways, you will find more depth and versatility in your superpowers coming online. Sound exciting? For me it was, and if you are inspired to keep reading, I know you are a part of a special class of compassionate warriors called for an incredibly exciting experience in this life.

If it feels a bit daunting, that is perfectly normal. This is a new game, a new experience, and it takes at least twenty times of doing something to start to be proficient at it. We will progress slowly as each quest builds on one another.

I STRONGLY suggest that you clear one mission a day, at the most two if you are feeling confident in each new concept. This is to prevent burning out and to give your body a chance to integrate the upgrades you are activating within you.

Before we get started, it's important to give gratitude to the teachers who have helped make this book possible.

This wisdom is not just my own, it is built off of the teachings of Dr. Joe Dispenza, the visionary guru Osho, the immaculate teacher Drunvalo Melchizedek and his devout student Iryna Eysmont, Deepak Chopra, Dr. Paul Drouin, Dr. Amit Goswami, Mindvalley's Vishen Lakhiani and Jeffrey Allen, Breath Master's Brian Kelly, Reiki master Brian Brunius, as well as principles supported by ancient teachings of the Amazonia and Buddhism.

The incredible stories of how all of these teachers have come to me over the past decade will unfold as the story does. But let's go to your first quest and discover what your Unique Attributes are!

QUEST 1 - CHARACTER CREATION SEQUENCE

Okay! It's the fun part of every role-playing game: time to build your character. In this case, since we are already playing the game of life, let's uncover our character attributes.

How will we do this? Throwback to when we used to play MS DOS RPG games like *Ultima*. This is a bit more fun and interactive with questions geared to give insight as to what characteristics you have used to advance through this life.

If you are familiar with the Myers-Briggs test, it has a series of questions that are related to archetypes. The activity goes through two fun quests connected with a guided meditation to correlate them. Let's prepare for the journey. What are your Unique Attribute Categories?

The same as any RPG, Strength, Dexterity (Flexibility), Intelligence, Wisdom/Vision, Constitution/Endurance, Charisma. These may seem self-explanatory, but as every game is unique, the loose categorization of each is as follows:

- Strength - Your physical strength and propensity to use prowess in this area to move through challenging situations. This number would be high if you are typically a leader in your group and find yourself being the "tip" of the spear in most group challenges.

- Dexterity - Your ability to be flexible in moving through life's challenges. This number would be high if you lean on your ability to see the big picture from a distance when moving through challenges. You may not be the leader of a group, but you provide great support.
- Intelligence - The Donatello of the group, pure intelligence and ability to solve puzzles of logic and knowledge faster than others. This number will be high for you if you lean on the power of your brain to move through life's challenges and may be described as "the smartest person" someone might know.
- Wisdom - Intelligence guided by experiences. This number will be high if you are able to take your experiences and gain a deeper meaning from them to guide you through life's challenges.
- Constitution - This is your resilience, in this case, your physical, emotional, spiritual, and intellectual resilience. This will be high if you are able to move through any challenge through sheer willpower and are a support for your friends through their own difficulties.
- Charisma - This is your ability to influence situational circumstances to reach your desired outcome. This will be high if you are extremely likable and, in any situation, feel you can orchestrate the chaos in a way that benefits your cause without getting flustered.

The caveat before starting this quest is to be BRUTALLY honest with yourself. Trust the heart, not what you "want" to be. The more honest you are with this exam from start to finish, the clearer your starting point will be. This journey is not for the faint of heart, as it has taken me years to uncover and unlock the hundreds of levels within myself. But I've found, without fail, that the more authentic and vulnerable I can be with myself, the faster I'm able to level up.

The key to growth is to first meet ourselves where we are at.

Make sure you have a set of headphones for the guided meditation/journey between each quest and be in a stable place where you can enjoy it.

MISSION 1: GAME OF LIFE CHARACTER CREATION

"In order for a seed to fully embody its purpose, it must come completely undone. The shell cracks, its insides come out, and everything changes. To those who don't understand transformation, this might look like complete destruction."
~Cynthia Occelli

Some may remember *Metroid Prime* or *Metroid: Zero Mission*, where Samus begins with an array of powerful abilities before a tragic event causes her to lose all her weapons and gifts. She then embarks on a journey not only to regain these abilities, but also to learn new ways to use them. This is the journey we are taking.

How does this relate to the Occelli quote? Before a seed becomes a tree, its entire form must change, and if you want to bring the magic of your energetic spirit avatar into the physical realm, then you need to fully activate your V.I.S.A., which stands for **Vulnerability, Intuition, Service to Others, and Awareness**.

I know that there are plenty of questions, but just like any good game, there is guidance, step by step, so that your actions will help allay any confusion created by this new way of living. I ask for your trust to lean into areas of discomfort to learn some amazing new skills that you haven't used before.

Remember the excitement that gaming has brought you and the spark that is created by the idea that you can transfer this excitement fully into life.

If you love gaming like I did, and there was a shot at bringing its pure joy and excitement into real life, wouldn't you take that chance? If I'm wrong, science has proven that what I'm going to teach you will at least provide tools to regulate stress, improve your quality of life and increase its longevity; who doesn't want to live a longer, more fulfilled life?

But if I'm right? Well, then not only will you improve your quality of life, but you'll also unlock a whole new set of attributes and skills to assist you in this process. Your V.I.S.A. will be your passport to an energetic realm that has been beckoning to you since you were a child. One of the skills that might be at your disposal is clairvoyance, the ability to sense energy with our sight, or clairaudience, the ability to sense energy with our ears, and more. Who knows, you might even gain your own spirit animal companion to support you through life's tough challenges!

From someone who is living that life, I have to say, it's a lot of fun for my wife and me.

But before you ask, how do I improve my Vulnerability, Intuition, Service to Others, or Awareness?

We first must calibrate ourselves in this game of life to build experience in these attributes and unlock their skill trees.

Excited? Let's jump into your first mission in the LTUVG App and jump into this epic adventure.

If you still haven't activated your free access to the companion app, use this QR Code, or go to (www.ltuvg.com) and use the code: LEVELUPMYLIFE for lifetime access to the missions required to beat the book.

Mission 1 Activated
Open the LTUVG App and access Mission 1:
Game of Life Character Creation

QUEST 2 - CALIBRATING YOUR CONTROLLER

This next quest is a fun way of unlocking a tool that has been with you from birth. It's what let everyone around you know you were officially in the game of life. It's also something that most people pay little attention to and take for granted. Our breath. It is our breath that is the key to controlling ourselves in life.

I'll ask a leading question. Do you want to button mash your way through life? Taking your chances with how you'll react in any situation, especially those that trigger you?

For those who don't know what a button masher is, these are the people who didn't know how to play games like *Super Smash Bros.* or *Mortal Kombat* and just press the direction pad and action buttons randomly hoping to win.

In gaming, the consequences of button mashing are minimal. You just won't improve at that given game. In life, however, button mashing has dire consequences. It means playing the same levels over and over again, with limited, or regressing progression.

Have you ever felt that as life's gotten tougher, you haven't leveled up with the increased degree of difficulty? Do you feel like there are areas in your life that stay the same, regardless of how hard you try to improve it? Like you're living in a loop of pain and suffering?

If so, you are most likely button mashing your way through life. Or at least in that area (or stage) of your life.

Don't fret though, because this upcoming mission will transform your life by allowing you to control yourself better, especially in trigger moments, so that you no longer guess your way through daily challenges!

I can share with you the science behind how fast breathing reflects being in a state of arousal or stress, and how slow breathing reflects being in a calmer state of peace or joy. But I'd rather you experience it for yourself.

Let's try something. Take fifteen fast breaths, in and out of your mouth, and think of something that makes you upset. It could be someone who hurt you or a painful life situation. Make yourself a promise not to become the emotion, just breathe fast, and feel the emotion in your body. Do it now.

Okay, now that you are in an aroused state, observe how you are breathing. It's probably a fast inhale, and a short exhale, possibly in and out of the chest. This is an activated state where the Sympathetic Nervous System (SNS) is aroused. When we are in Freeze, Fight, Flight, or Fawn, this is the physiological state we are in.[1]

---

[1] Porges, S. W. (2007). The polyvagal perspective. Biological Psychology, 74(2), 116-143. https://doi.org/10.1016/j.biopsycho.2006.06.009

Now let's release that state, breathe into the belly, in through the nose for five seconds, and out for five seconds, through the nose. You can also make it for four seconds if five is too difficult. Repeat this breathing pattern fifteen to twenty times. While you are doing this, think of something for which you are grateful. Your friends, family, nature, your pets, something that reflects gratitude in your life.

When you're done, come back here.

How are you feeling? What is your breathing pattern like naturally? Is it a smooth inhale with a little longer exhale? This is a more natural breathing pattern that is activating the Parasympathetic Nervous System (PNS) for rest and relaxation.[2]

Did you notice that by simply changing your breathing pattern to slow controlled breaths, you were able to shift your emotional state? Research has shown that there's a bidirectional relationship between breathing patterns and emotions. Not only do our emotions influence our breathing, but deliberately changing our breathing can also affect our emotional state.[3]

In day-to-day life, your breathing pattern usually emulates your emotions. When you feel a specific emotion, your breathing pattern follows suit. Often this is an unconscious process, but by becoming aware of it,

---

[2] Gerritsen, R. J. S., & Band, G. P. H. (2018). Breath of Life: The Respiratory Vagal Stimulation Model of Contemplative Activity. Frontiers in Human Neuroscience, 12, 397. https://doi.org/10.3389/fnhum.2018.00397

[3] Philippot, P., Chapelle, G., & Blairy, S. (2002). Respiratory feedback in the generation of emotion. Cognition & Emotion, 16(5), 605-627. https://doi.org/10.1080/02699930143000392

we can learn to exert more control over our emotional states.

How many times have you reacted when "triggered" by an emotion of anxiety, anger, disappointment, jealousy, or fear when life comes at you fast? Only to apologize later for your reaction because you weren't in full control of yourself. Button mashing again, whoops.

I used to be like this, and it wasn't until I started practicing breathwork that I started taking back control of my "Player One" in the video game of my life.

As a Breath Master, I have been holding a men's circle for the past two years with a divine group of men living life with more awareness and control of themselves. We go through fifteen to thirty minutes of breathwork every two weeks. Recently, a member shared a story about how his partner tended to lose her ability to control her emotions when she got upset. She was aware that she shouldn't be upset, but she couldn't detach herself from the emotion. It's what we will call being "triggered."

The last time that this happened, my friend had an epiphany. "Would you be open to trying breathwork?" he asked her.

"I'll try anything," she replied, exhausted and frustrated by the continuous loops.

After about five minutes of breathwork, not only did she let go of the anger she was feeling, but she also understood where the anger was coming from. From a feeling of not being heard or appreciated. To which my friend apologized and shared that her opinion was valid, and he wanted to incorporate her vision into their project together.

I call this a Collective Gem of Understanding, because it allowed my friend's partner to understand why she was getting angry, empowering her to communicate her needs, which then allowed her partner to understand how to support her better in the future. A win-win for everyone! Her leveling up resulted in the collective, their relationship, leveling up.

This is the power of breathwork. This is the power of calibrating ourselves in the game of life. To stop unconsciously button mashing through life, as my friend's partner found herself doing.

In the upcoming mission, I will show you the simple exercise that she did to center and calibrate herself so she could communicate her needs to her partner.

Another way to think of this breathwork is that it calibrates our controller. Would you ever want to play a video game where your controller wasn't fully synced to the screen? As a gamer, I hope the answer is no. Especially when playing challenging levels, your controller needs to be calibrated. If your breathing pattern is that of anger, fear, or anxiety and your SNS is hyper-focused on specific objectives, it compromises your overall judgement.

You may feel like you are performing at a high level, and maybe you can for a short period of time, but it's unsustainable because your screen is becoming uncalibrated. Your emotions affect your judgment and skew the ability to control yourself. You're "triggered."

So, what is the breathing pattern that allows us to, in an instant, recalibrate our screen?

Have you ever played *Call of Duty*, or any game as a sniper? When you aim at your target, considering the wind, the distance, etc.—what is the last thing you do before pulling the trigger? You take a controlled breath in, pause your breath, pull the trigger, and release.

In real life, when Navy Seals are in high-stress situations, they use a similar breathing technique, based in ancient yogi traditions, to calm the nervous system and improve performance.

This calibration process is called "Box Breathing."

So go to your LTUVG app and select the next mission to calibrate yourself. Hurry, you're leaking XP all over the place!

MISSION 2: MASTER YOUR BREATH, MASTER YOUR LIFE

Mission 2 Activated
Open the LTUVG App and access Mission 2:
Master Your Breath, Master Your Life

How was that experience? Did you feel your stress in the body just melt away? Let this be your go-to breathwork in life until we develop other tools. Now it's time to earn some more XP with our first Journal Activity!

Think of journaling, even if it feels like a chore, as a way to boost your experience points. There are multiple studies that show that for us to remember any new piece of information, we need to digest it three different ways: reading, experiencing, and writing. As you read this book, you are gaining XP once. By doing each exercise, you gain XP twice. Lastly, by journaling, you gain XP thrice and create the opportunity for a special bonus! When we journal in a "stream of consciousness" method, we tap into the subconscious mind. This gives us XP for our awareness and allows for our subconscious experiences to come to the surface. Then, when we come back and read that journal, it gives us the opportunity to relive aspects of our experience again, activating more experience points!

What is the name of the game? To gain enough XP so that we can level up and attain Gems of Understanding, aka, "aha" moments. This all cycles and supports our ability to remain calibrated in life because each GOU deactivates a trigger within us. Think of your journal, whether it's a book or in a journal app, as the journal in any RPG like *Uncharted*. It will hold experiences that act as clues to help unlock future levels within yourself that you aren't aware of yet.

The Journal Activity for today will only be for two to three minutes on how it felt! A mini warmup to show the fun and benefits. If you "don't know how it felt", write that too, and why! There are no wrong answers in these exercises. There is no failing, just that we try, and trust that the fun will come to us.

After the journaling, if you've binged this chapter, I suggest taking a break for the day, give yourself full gratitude and congratulations for getting this far, and come back refreshed tomorrow so you can learn to USE your controller, now that you can calibrate it.

QUEST 3 - ACTIVATING YOUR CONTROLLER

Congratulations! After many years, you now know how to calibrate yourself in the game of life. You'd think that society would have provided a handbook for at least this part, don't you?

Speaking of limitations that society wants us to stay in, here's another important announcement:

Be gentle with yourself,
during this activation process.

You might have thoughts of self-doubt, anxiety, frustration, guilt, possibly shame while you take more control of consciousness. These thoughts are perfectly natural. Why? Because we live in a world of TikTok, Instagram, comparing our experiences to others, thinking we should be "further" along than we are based on our perception of other people's lives (that often aren't even accurate).

"Comparison is the death of Joy."
~Mark Twain

Eckhart Tolle elaborates on this idea confirming that comparison with others either feeds pride, making us feel better than others, or envy, instilling a feeling of being lesser than others. Both lead to suffering.[4] Society feeds us these comparisons to create negative self-talk within ourselves: "we're not good enough", "we will never be ___," "other people have the things that we want."

As we continue to calibrate and become more aware of ourselves as we are, these thoughts may come to the surface. When I say "be gentle" with yourself, I mean give yourself grace. Remember, these thoughts are not your fault, and it is also your responsibility to understand where they come from. As thoughts arise and you feel a negative emotion attaching, use your first tool, the box breath, and see if some clarity comes to you as to why. If it doesn't come, that's okay, this will become accessible to you at a higher-level skill. We'll start to build some Universal Attributes at later levels to help uncover it.

If a negative thought or emotion emerges, begin the practice of doing three to five box breaths, and saying three to five positive things about yourself. It can be spoken mentally or out loud. As an example, if you are doing a meditation exercise and encounter a thought such as "I can't do this", counter that with "I can do this," "I am able to observe my thoughts," "I'm observing them right now!"

---

[4] Tolle, Eckhart. *A New Earth: Awakening to Your Life's Purpose*. Penguin, 2005.

If you have resistance to saying positive things about yourself, then that's a sign that you NEED to do this if you want to level up your life. Starting this process now will only make the next levels easier, because self-love holds some of the biggest XP bonuses that life has to offer.

Studies have shown that one negative thought can drain your energy, but if you say five positive things, it will counterbalance the one negative thought and feed your energy.[5] We'll cover this science later in the book when we go over energy centers (or chakras) in the body. For the time being, think of the childhood story, *The Little Engine That Could*. It repeated the mantra "I think I can" repeatedly, over and over again, and sure enough, it got over that hill.

One of the first goals of this book is to help you become aware of the subconscious thoughts that are holding you back. Did you know that by the age of thirty-five, most humans average 60,000 thoughts a day?[6] Yes, per day. How many of those thoughts do you think are conscious thoughts?

Maybe you're thinking half of them...no, way off. 10k? Nah, it's still lower. Maybe 5k? Still too high, but you are closer. The number is 5 percent, a whopping 3,000 of the 60k thoughts that cycle through our mind are actually conscious. Before you freak out, as many do in

---

[5] Shine Team. (n.d.). Challenge Your Negative Thinking with the 5:1 Ratio. Shine. https://advice.theshineapp.com/articles/challenge-your-negative-thinking-with-the-5-1-ratio/

[6] "Programmed to be human?" https://www.ncbi.nlm.nih.gov/pmc/articles/PMC3950304/ & Brain Facts by Cleveland Clinic Foundation https://healthybrains.org/brain-facts/

the corporate workshops we offer, I want to allay any fears that are popping up. It's also completely normal, as our bodies are designed that way.

What is abnormal, however, is that according to a National Science Foundation study in 2005, 80 percent of those thoughts are considered negative thought patterns. Either memories from past events, things we've seen on the news, or general limiting beliefs that have stuck with us through our lives, that have informed our subconscious of how to think.

Why am I sharing this information with you? I'll answer that question with another question.

Don't you want to know what those 60,000 thoughts are thinking? Are your thoughts mostly negative like the study found in most people? What if while you are trying to accomplish your goals in life, your thoughts are subconsciously undermining your own growth? Wouldn't you want to know?

The good news is, in this next quest we'll look under the hood of our own subconscious and find out. The only way to do this is through meditation or journeying. We have to become the observer of our own thoughts without associating with them. To unlock the door to these practices, we need to practice breathwork to get our bodies in a state where we can access these states of consciousness easier.

As we begin practicing breathwork, and it will be challenging at first, remember that this is the fastest way to access our subconscious mind. To quiet the analytical mind so that we can open a portal to the roughly 57,000 other thoughts we have daily.

This is effectively what journeying is. The ability to enter and explore our subconscious mind and observe and interact with our thoughts. It's a shamanism practice that is ages old and will become an ability that you will rely on often to understand more what's going on in and around you.

We have already calibrated our controller through breathwork, and we need to know how to activate our bodies through different breathwork patterns. Remember that by changing our breathing pattern, we can change our emotional state. We create space in our bodies so that we can observe the emotion we are embodying at that moment and choose whether we want to embody a different emotion. Maybe move from a state of anger to compassion, from fear to courage, from sadness to motivation.

To understand this concept a bit more, have you ever thought about what an emotion was? In simplistic terms, our emotion is a feeling that we choose to embody, that informs us of what type of experience we are having. For example, I have a friend who works for a highly valued (in the billions) company. He's been there for a couple years, and recently when I met up with him, I was telling him about this part of the book, about how our emotions determine our experience. He laughed and made an immediate connection with our emotions and how the same experience can create very different reactions in people, depending on their level of awareness and gratitude.

His lived example of this involved him receiving some AirPods from his company as a gift. They gave them to all the employees. My buddy, we'll call him Jean, was ecstatic! He'd been using wired headphones for years and never even knew what AirPods were like. He was so grateful to his company. He soon found out that he probably was the only one who felt this way. Everyone else felt scammed. The headphones were the v1 of AirPods. AirPods are on v3 now. What his company actually was clearing up closet space and probably using the equipment as a tax write-off!

While my buddy might feel more grateful to his company and want to stay longer, if you were not in a good place with the company, this "false" gift might drive someone else to be upset and look for another job. A bit dramatic in the latter example, but you understand the point. The same event happens, but different emotions create a different decision tree and experience. This goes for experiences that might be more intense and serious.

Let's say I think I lost $10,000. A bit less trivial. I might be angry, disappointed in myself, or worse. This emotion is telling me that I'm having a pretty shitty life experience. Then as I'm coming back home, I find a hundred-dollar bill on the ground... How do I respond?

I might respond with frustration at the Universe. Like is this some cosmic joke? I lost $10,000 and you gave me $100 back? I then spend the rest of the evening obsessing over finding my money and wasting time I could have spent with my wife and amazing cats. This would define a very negative life experience where I was embodying emotions of anger, sadness, disappointment, and feelings of lack.

Let's say the same situation happened, and instead of responding with anger and desperation... I come home upset, but trust that the money will show up somewhere else. As I approach my door, I see that same hundred-dollar bill. This time though, I see this as a sign that everything will be okay.

Full of gratitude for the positive omen of finding the hundred dollars, I decide to take my wife out for dinner. While at dinner, we meet a beautiful couple that is in the philanthropic space. We make an authentic connection, and they inform us of a new $50,000 grant they are releasing. We later go on to secure this grant to help support individuals in need. What an amazing blessing!

From observing the emotions of gratitude, appreciation, resilience, and forgiveness, one might say I had an incredibly challenging, yet amazing day! To top it off, when I get back in the car to drive home, my wife opens the glove compartment to put in the new couple's business card and lo and behold, she sees the envelope of money I misplaced! This may or may not be based on a true story.

Imagine how much worse I might have felt if I had gone the negative emotion route, sulked about losing money and neglecting my family, only to find the money later?

Instead, I acknowledged my anger, released it, stayed present and positive, and made:

Lemonade, out of a lemony situation.

It exemplifies the concept that your emotions can upgrade or downgrade your experience, regardless of what is happening to you. This is why the resilience of kids living with pediatric cancer is so inspirational. Their survivorship rate is 20 percent higher than adults[7] because of their increased resilience. I believe this is because they maintain a positive attitude, because they still have the innocence and hope of their inner child.

This is why we are on a mission to rescue our inner child. We can ALWAYS choose what type of emotion we are attaching to, by taking deep breaths and raising our awareness, and by using the tools that we are activating in this book. I say always, and I also acknowledge that:

While observing our emotions is a simple process, it may not be easy.

We can be more aware of our emotional attachments in the heat of our emotional days through the daily practice of breathwork in the calm of the morning or peace of the evening.

Our goal is to get to the point where we can observe all interactions as conversations with other non-player

---

[7] https://pcrf-kids.org/2024/03/27/understanding-the-differences-between-pediatric-adult-cancers/

characters (NPCs) in your favorite role-playing games. If you played *Knights of the Old Republic*, *Fable*, *Skyrim*, or others, you'll recognize this concept. When there is an interaction and you can choose a positive response, negative response, or neutral response, it has an impact on your conversation, as well as the outcome of your game.

By building our breath control, we create the opportunity to see these response screens in our daily life and start to choose different emotions than we usually might. As a result, we can avoid pitfalls of old situations that used to "trigger" us in the levels of our life. We can instead choose an elevated emotion like patience and compassion to clear these challenges with awareness and wisdom. When you reach this point in life, take it from me, life becomes much more fun and engaging because you are gaining more and more XP! Challenges in life will empower you, much like the feeling of beating a challenging level in a video game.

MISSION 3: CONTROLLING YOUR CONTROLLER - PNS VS SNS

Have you ever immersed yourself in the magical world of Hyrule in The Legend of Zelda? In games like Breath of the Wild and Tears of the Kingdom, health and stamina are crucial for successfully navigating these expansive worlds. Link, the protagonist, can fully explore the world from the beginning, limited only by his stamina bar that depletes as he runs and climbs the towering mountain ranges.

We have a similar system for our own stamina and resilience, called the autonomic nervous system (ANS). The ANS regulates our body's ability to react to danger or to rest and restore[8]. To maintain balance, our ANS has designed an ingenious system that works with every inhale and exhale we make, primarily through the vagus nerve.

When we exhale, our body experiences respiratory sinus arrhythmia (RSA). A bundle of nerves in the vagus nerve, called the nucleus ambiguus, slows the heartbeat during exhalation and activates our parasympathetic nervous system (PNS)[9]. Think of this like the brake on a car, or in Zelda terms, pausing to allow your stamina bar to increase. Once our 'stamina bar' is filled, we inhale, and the body releases the "vagal brake," allowing the heart rate to increase. Our body also activates our sympathetic nervous system (SNS) when we inhale, responding to the incoming energy and oxygen. This creates a seesaw effect within our body's equilibrium.

With every breath, your body balances between the SNS and PNS, between action and rest. It's similar to the balance between running and resting in Zelda to maintain the energy needed to save Hyrule.

What happens if you don't have a balanced inhale-to-exhale ratio? Your metaphorical stamina bar depletes,

---

[8] McCorry, L. K. (2007). Physiology of the Autonomic Nervous System. American Journal of Pharmaceutical Education, 71(4), 78.

[9] Yasuma, F., & Hayano, J. (2004). Respiratory sinus arrhythmia: Why does the heartbeat synchronize with respiratory rhythm? Chest, 125(2), 683-690.

leaving you without the resources to overcome life's challenges.

In a nutshell, this is what we are doing to our bodies unconsciously when we are in constant states of anxiety, stress, and fight or flight. Our inhales are fast and shallow, and our exhales are even shorter or nonexistent. That's right, sometimes we are unconsciously holding our breath rather than fully exhaling. This can lead to dorsal vagal shutdown, where our nucleus ambiguus no longer functions due to constant stimulation of the vagus nerve. This often results in health issues such as hypertension, inflammation, and more.[10]

If this is you, it's okay.
Nearly 20 percent of Americans suffer with anxiety, 60 percent of whom don't seek help with it.[11]

To provide tools for reducing and releasing anxiety, here are two deep breathing exercises that will not only reduce stress but also improve focus and help release 70% of the toxins from our body.[12]

First, we are going to learn how to balance our bodies equilibrium with what is called "Coherent Breathing."

---

[10] Porges, S. W. (2007). The polyvagal perspective. Biological Psychology, 74(2), 116-143.
[11] McPhillips, D. (2023, January 24). *Anxiety Statistics: Facts You Need To Know.* Forbes Health. Retrieved September 15, 2024, from https://www.forbes.com/health/mind/anxiety-statistics/
[12] Northrup C. (2006). Moving Beyond Cancer

It's designed to create homeostasis in the body by activating our PNS with slow, controlled breaths.

So, head to the LTUVG app and select today's mission to unlock your second skill.

Mission 3a Activated
Open the LTUVG App and access Mission 3a:
Co-Breath for Rest

Amazing work! Coherent Breathing is something you can do at any moment in life you remember to do it. We'll call it Co-Breath, because it is your co-pilot that keeps you centered while life becomes turbulent.

A good combo, especially if you notice you are in a hyper-aroused state, is to practice 3-4 box breaths, followed by 5 minutes of Co-Breath. It works like a charm to calm the alarm systems of the body. Improving your ability to navigate the most difficult challenges in life with acceptance and humility.

Now, let's talk about upgrading your emotional regulation through CO2 tolerance. Euphoric breathing, a technique that involves controlled hyperventilation followed by breath holds, can increase your body's CO2 tolerance.

This is crucial because higher CO2 tolerance levels correlate with better emotional regulation and awareness[13]. Think of it as adding more units to your metaphorical stamina bar in life.

---

[13] Zaccaro, A., Piarulli, A., Laurino, M., Garbella, E., Menicucci, D., Neri, B., & Gemignani, A. (2018). How Breath-Control Can Change Your Life: A Systematic

Interestingly, studies have shown that even in patients missing part of their amygdala (the brain's fear center), injecting CO2 triggered a fear response, highlighting the deep connection between CO2 levels and our emotional state[14]. By increasing our CO2 tolerance, we can reduce how often we're "triggered" emotionally, giving us more resilience when approaching aroused states.

You can find this next breathwork session in the LTUVG app in part 2 of Mission 3.

Mission 3b Activated

Open the LTUVG App and access Mission 3b:

Euphoric Breathing for Expansion

Doesn't it feel empowering to have two skills at your disposal to control yourself better in life? I know what you might be thinking—what about the brain? Isn't this how we control ourselves in life? Yes, that is how we physically move our bodies and process our environment, even how we tell ourselves to breathe. But we are learning how to control the FULL body within the game. This includes emotions, energy, and connection to your higher self. In that sense, the brain can actually limit this connection.

Review on Psycho-Physiological Correlates of Slow Breathing. Frontiers in Human Neuroscience, 12, 353.

[14] Feinstein, J. S., Buzza, C., Hurlemann, R., Follmer, R. L., Dahdaleh, N. S., Coryell, W. H., ... & Wemmie, J. A. (2013). Fear and panic in humans with bilateral amygdala damage. Nature Neuroscience, 16(3), 270-272.

"The brain is an amazing servant, but a terrible master."

More on this later. Trust me, this is how I've been able to release my anger and fears and manifest my dreams of making millions in finance so I can start my own nonprofit helping millions of people heal themselves. I've manifested the millions and the nonprofit, The Warrior Sanctuary, and I'm connecting with thousands of brave souls like yourself, hopefully more.

What do you want to accomplish in life? The bigger the goal is, the more leaning into your breath will help, no exceptions. If you want to go about life how you have been, only using a small percentage of your abilities in this world and getting the same results from the pain and suffering you are going through, I support that as well. I will always encourage reflection and recommitment to why you are here, because I cannot force you to do the work, which is up to you. What I can do is promise that the more you lean into your V.I.S.A., the more you will be rewarded on the other side. Are you still in? Okay, then let's add onto these building blocks to continue exploring this new way of engaging with life!

Level 1 Recap:

- Physical Skills Unlocked:
    - Journaling
    - Box Breathing
    - Euphoric Breathwork
    - Coherent Breathwork (Co-Breath)

LEVEL 2

ENTERING THE SUBTLE ENERGY REALM

Welcome to Level 2 of Life the Ultimate Video Game! Before we jump into this chapter, please make sure that you've entered your first mandatory online "mission log" entry. As we covered in the Introduction of this inspiration manual, reflection and community are key for successfully making it through this journey. And we want you to "beat" this game and live a happier, more fulfilled life.

By sharing your experience with others, and commenting on other's experiences, it creates a giant LAN party through space and time, supporting you along the way. As an avid Destiny player, I loved seeing others running around accomplishing their missions while I farmed and grinded for my own objectives. Completing the writing prompts will also give you extra XP every time you reflect on these new experiences. So, if you haven't entered your mission log for Level 1, do it now so you can jump into the next quest seamlessly.

Now we are ready to discuss how to activate and build up our V.I.S.A. attributes so that we can bring our spirit avatar's subtle energy abilities to life in the material realm. If you've already completed the initial quest, you should know what your Unique Spirit Avatar is and the starting badge you have earned. The goal is to build out every attribute in our V.I.S.A. through these quests and activities that will expand your ability to access and master the subtle energy realm around you.

Your V.I.S.A., or Universal Attributes, are exactly that—attributes that are universally accessible to help guide us through the game of life. Unlike our Unique Attributes, which are predisposed to the personalities that we come into this world with, Universal Attributes are an even playing field for everyone. I refer to them as your V.I.S.A. Attributes because they are your passport to entering the subtle energy realm. In entering this realm, it allows you to imbue your Unique Attributes with special abilities.

Before we can get to this exciting part, let's discuss the definitions of each of these attributes so you can begin to build them up!

<u>Vulnerability</u>: Our ability to surrender in any given moment to the experience we are having—good, bad, neutral—and embody our most authentic self regardless of, or because of, traumatic events in our lives.

Intuition: Our ability to listen to our higher/natural self at any given moment to receive messages from the subtle energy realm (I know, I'm explaining it soon!).

Service to Others: Our ability to offer our gifts in the service of helping others vs being in the service of self. Think of Jesus, Buddha, Mother Teresa, Martin Luther King Jr., and Gandhi. These individuals have left a lasting mark for positive change in the world, many sacrificing their lives for the greater good. They also had incredible gifts to create healing through touch, action, words, or all of the above.

Awareness: Our ability to be present at any given moment. Or rather hit the escape (ESC) button, as I call it. Entering Elevated States of Consciousness (ESC) to slow down time and get a bird's-eye view of what is happening. Giving us the ability to observe our experiences as a movie and us the audience. Unattached to right or wrong, just in observance of how to navigate the situation for the highest good of yourself and all involved.

Before we start the missions to unlock these attributes within you, let's dive a little further into what the "subtle energy realm" is.

As you probably know, we are made up of atoms, billions of them. Something to the order of 10^{27}.[15] Within those atoms, matter, the energy that we connect with on a daily basis, only takes up a minuscule fraction of that space. According to physicist Nassim Haramein's

---

[15] Villanueva, J. C. (2009). How Many Atoms Are There in the Universe? Universe Today.

research, the proton-to-electron mass ratio suggests that matter accounts for <.00004% of the total volume of an atom, while the remaining ~99.99996 % is a "quantum vacuum," or probability matrix, that matter can manifest in.[16]

Our five senses of touch, sight, hearing, taste, and feeling can only sense the small fraction of matter that, as Einstein stated, slows down for us to interact with.[17] The subtle energy realm is the realm that encapsulates the vast majority of space around us and our Universe.

The subtle energy realm includes our thoughts, emotions, dreams, and the infinite possibilities that life can flow in. It includes our energy field, created by the biophotons that make up the building blocks of our bodies.[18]

Said another way, anyone who is familiar with RPGs is also familiar with the concept of mana, the unseen energy that any magic user calls upon to cast magic spells. Even battle mages use mana to infuse their weapons with magic as well.

The subtle energy realm is similar to mana in RPGs. It represents an unseen but vital force that influences our physical, emotional, and spiritual well-being. Just as managing mana is crucial for a character's performance,

---

[16] Haramein, N., Brown, W. D., & Val Baker, A. (2016). The Unified Spacememory Network: from Cosmogenesis to Consciousness. Journal of NeuroQuantology, 14(4).
[17] Einstein, A. (1905). On the Electrodynamics of Moving Bodies. Annalen der Physik, 17, 891-921.
[18] Popp, F. A., et al. (1988). Biophoton emission: New evidence for coherence and DNA as source. Cell Biophysics, 6(1), 33-52.

understanding and balancing our subtle energy can enhance our overall health and capabilities.[19]

Think of your Unique Attributes as your physical skills, while your Universal Attributes allow access to imbue these skills with additional energy. Before we start thinking that this is going to get super complicated, don't worry, this instruction manual is designed to demystify the ability to access this subtle energy realm.

By simply improving your V.I.S.A., you will unlock this new skill tree system! Together, we are going to focus on these four Attributes for the next thirty to sixty days as you work through this instruction manual, so that you will not only improve these skills, but also dramatically improve the quality of your life!

Just as any skilled mage must learn to harness and channel magical energies, we too must activate our V.I.S.A. to tap into the subtle energy realm. Without this crucial connection, our attempts to influence the world around us would be as ineffective as casting spells without mana. Think about it – imagine if, when Gandalf said, "You shall not pass!" that all that happened was the staff went into the ground and went **thud*. The Balrog would have laughed and wiped out the entire Fellowship of the Ring! There would have been no books, no movie, and no wizard!

Another way to think of subtle energies is akin to the subtitles of a foreign movie.

---

[19] Popp, F. A., et al. (1988). Biophoton emission: New evidence for coherence and DNA as source. Cell Biophysics, 6(1), 33-52.

Subtitles require us to put all our attention toward the TV show or movie to understand what is going on. While we read the words, we also pay attention to the body language, the intonation, the subtle energies that the person is subconsciously communicating with the other person. Studies have actually shown that communication is only 7 percent of what is actually being said, while the rest is body language (55 percent) and intonation (38 percent)[20]. Subtitles in a movie give you context to the subtle energy that you are subconsciously observing with your intuition and awareness, gathering information on what is happening in any given scene.

Continuing with this analogy, subtitles make the content of a movie accessible to a broader audience. For example, if you are watching a movie in Spanish, with English subtitles, and you only speak English, the subtitles allow you to understand what is clearly going on. But if you understand body language, intonation, and other nonverbal cues, you can probably watch a movie without subtitles and understand a large part of what is going on. Maybe not granular details, but enough to follow the plot and connect with the characters. This is also true for someone who is attuned to the subtle energy of the Universe.

In fact, we have a friend and mentor, Itzhak Beery, who is an elder shaman who works with the subtle energies of the Universe to diagnose psychosomatic illnesses with his clients and help them heal themselves. He has

---

[20] Mehrabian, A. (1971). Silent Messages: Implicit Communication of Emotions and Attitudes. Belmont, CA: Wadsworth.

been practicing for over twenty-five years and is the first person who opened the subtle energy realm to me over ten years ago. He guided me in what is called a Soul Retrieval so that I could heal misunderstood ancestral trauma. A story for another time, but his gifts are a testament to his mastery of navigating the subtle energy realms.

However, despite Itzhak's decades spent traveling to South America, he speaks very little Spanish. He was trained and ordained by an Ecuadorian shaman who doesn't speak English and has built partnerships with shamans of the Amazon who speak their native tongue of Quechua and Safiki. Itzhak speaks none of those other languages. It's as if he is navigating a foreign flick without the subtitles, with a full understanding of what is going on. We have seen him listen to and communicate with them doing intimate soul work, simply using body language and communicating through the subtle energy realm.

It doesn't mean that he doesn't turn on the subtitles to discuss details like time, place, etc. There is a translator on hand for these things. But when we think about "what is the subtle energy realm," we can think of it as the underlying information that supports the experience in the material realm or the realm of definitions.

This is the realm of what we already "know," or at least think that we know. If you have studied the brain, you know that it is scientifically designed to predict what is going to happen next. It utilizes old experiences and our belief system to predict what will happen in any given situation, even if an alternate answer is obvious.

Part of this has to do with the fact that our conscious mind only can process 30-40 bits of information per second, while our subconscious/unconscious brain processes nearly 11 million bits of info per second.[21] As a result, our brain resorts to predicting outcomes before they happen.[22]

For example, have you ever heard of the story about the tragic plane accident with a pilot and his son? The father didn't survive, but his son did. In critical condition, when the doctor saw the boy, they said, "I can't operate on him, he's, my son." How is this possible?

Our mind might go to the possibility of the son having two dads before realizing that the doctor was his mother.

It's so obvious it's a bit frustrating that our minds are subconsciously programmed to think that women aren't doctors, or pilots, for that matter. This also applies to our own life situations. We consciously or subconsciously put limitations on what we can accomplish in our lives based on what society tells us is possible.

This is a reason why, before amazing feats like the sub-four-minute mile were run, or Tony Hawk completed a 1080 skateboarding, it was thought impossible. Ironically, as soon as Roger Bannister broke the 4-

---

[21] Zimmermann, M. (1989). The nervous system in the context of information theory. In Human physiology (pp. 166-173). Springer, Berlin, Heidelberg.

[22] Friston, K. (2010). The free-energy principle: a unified brain theory? *Nature Reviews Neuroscience*, 11(2), 127–138. doi:10.1038/nrn2787

minute barrier, multiple people, objectively less athletic than the pioneers of the feat, also surpassed this goal. People thought it wasn't possible, until one person's belief that it was possible proved it could be done. In just 70 years since, over 1700 people have accomplished this feat.

This is why suspending disbelief is so crucial for you to unlock the skills I'm showing you in this book. For once you see that the subtle energy realm is real from your own experiences, your own belief system will expand exponentially.

Which leads me to the question: If matter is the realm of definitions, what is the world of subtle energy? I'll spare the suspense—subtle energy lives in the realm of possibilities.

What's amazing about the subtle energy realm is that as we become well versed in listening to and interacting with this realm, we can shift our material realm drastically. We can accomplish things that we once didn't think were possible.

We can break out of our current life situation that is full of stress, suffering, bad habits and less abundant than we deserve. Currently many of you are living your lives like it's a rerun of a TV show you've already seen before, half paying attention because you "know" what's going to happen next. What would happen if you began to pay full attention to your life? The experience points you need to level up your life are all around you. You have to open your mind to the possibility that other outcomes are available to you. That you deserve the best in life, and that you are worthy of this reality.

I was able to do this in my own life. I woke up one day and said, no more reruns! So, join me in this Imagination Realization revolution. Together, let's harness all the energy from our life experiences so that we can exponentially level up our life!

What do you say?

Do you want to stay in the loop of your life and make minimal progress every day? Or do you want to earn the most XP possible from each experience so you can massively accelerate your leveling up process? If the answer is yes to the latter, keep reading, and you will be rewarded.

Remember *The Matrix* scene with the kid and the bending spoon? It's not that we are bending reality with our own mind, but we are accepting that reality as we know it is not limited by the definitions of the material realm.

"Do not try to bend the spoon. That's impossible. Instead, only try to realize the truth: there is no spoon."

To step into this realm of possibilities, "suspend disbelief" long enough for your own experiences to inform you of these infinite possibilities.

It will be needed for the next quest, which is designed to activate and upgrade the first letter of your V.I.S.A. Your Vulnerability.

QUEST 4 - OPENING OUR HEARTS TO VULNERABILITY

One of the most intense games that I have played, which was adapted into a full-on series chronicling the emotional journey of Ellie and Joel, was *Last of Us*. Minor spoiler alert for anyone who has not seen either...Joel loses his daughter tragically in the beginning of the game as two police officers shoot and kill her, fearing she was already turning into a zombie.

While on the run for his survival, Joel meets a young girl named Ellie, who is in dire need of a protector. Joel begrudgingly fulfills this role, and as their journey unfolds, they must learn to rely on one another to survive and find a cure for this pandemic.

In the beginning of their relationship, Joel is cold and closed off to Ellie. He attempts to do all the fighting on his own, in a way to protect Ellie, but also to protect his own heart from additional pain. By keeping himself closed off emotionally from Ellie, he won't be attached to her if she dies in the ensuing battles to come. This is a very human reaction to insufferable loss. To close ourselves off when we can't endure any more pain. Much like not getting another pet after the loss of a long-lived friend.

What you learn throughout the game though, is that as Joel softens and makes himself vulnerable again, they can overcome bigger challenges. In fact, as their bond grows, these two strangers realize they have more in common with one another than at first meets the eye. I won't spoil any more of it for you if you haven't seen the end of the first game/season, but I highly recommend it. The story is a beautiful commentary on how vulnerability can benefit us individually and collectively as humanity.

"Vulnerability is the birthplace of love, belonging, joy, courage, empathy, and creativity. It is the source of hope, accountability, and authenticity."

Vulnerability is a superpower that you can choose to embody, or conversely, choose to close yourself off to. While it might feel safer not to be vulnerable, by doing so, we actually close off our hearts from growth. This is exhibited in Brené Brown's studies around living wholeheartedly. If you haven't heard of Brené Brown, she is a Ph.D. researcher and social worker who has spent the past two decades studying vulnerability, courage, shame, and empathy. In her book, *Gifts of Imperfection*, she discusses the ten guideposts of "Wholehearted Living," a concept that involves letting go of shame and cultivating vulnerability. To name a few, she found that people who let go of perfectionism, the need for certainty and comparison, to cultivate self-compassion, intuition and faith, and creativity, live a happier lifestyle.

It is through her studies and analysis of data via grounded theory, where she compiled over 10,000 case files and interviews of diverse groups of men and women ages eighteen to eighty, that she discovered the root of what "wholehearted living" taps into. In her book, *Daring Greatly*, she reveals that the key to transforming how we live our lives, for our highest good, is through the courage to be vulnerable. To be our most authentic selves in every moment of our lives, especially the ones where shame, scarcity, and the pain of loss arise.

I highly recommend diving into her books to help further understanding of this topic, but in this book, we heal and open our hearts through doing. We can teach ourselves anything by turning off the mind and surrendering the heart. Just as in any video game, one level unlocks another, and since intuition, service to others, and awareness are all guided by the heart, if we don't start with vulnerability, we aren't going to get very far on this journey, so let's jump in!

Remember your breath, so that whenever you feel the nerves locking up, use your box breathing exercise to take back control of yourself in this mission.

The first step in vulnerability is with ourselves. Vulnerability and honesty are very much aligned in that way. When we aren't comfortable being vulnerable and open with people, we often choose the vibration of being dishonest, and over time, we might tell a mistruth so often that it becomes our truth.

As we step into our full power, we must break down that layer, or those layers, that we have built between our true self, who we were born as, and any false selves we have created, also known as projections of the person we want others to see. It's fully natural to have shame around your true self, trust me.

As a biracial kid growing up in a racist area of Spokane, WA, I had plenty of identity issues that I had to accept and integrate back into myself. Between being too black to be accepted by white people, or not black enough to be accepted by black people, I had created numerous alter-egos by the time I was graduating from college. But every time that I healed a part of myself, just like Samus, I called back another gift of mine. One of those limiting beliefs I had was being a bad writer and look at me now!

Let's start you on this path of transformation with this simple exercise of self-acceptance and self-forgiveness. While I admit it's simple, it may be one of the most difficult things to do. That's why we are starting with it, because getting through this will open the door to your heart and amazing gifts that may have been dormant since childhood. A teacher once told me, if you are afraid of doing something, it means that you need to do it twice as much as those who hold no fear around it. If you have strong reservations about self-forgiveness, with love and compassion:

The magic you are looking for is in the work you are avoiding.

So, as you start to make progress in this one mission, you will see the beautiful benefits on the other side rapidly. That being said, I love you for being here, and you are an amazing being for even having the courage to make it this far, so if you struggle with this next quest, you are not alone, and I'm here to support you.

Let's go to the LTUVG app and start today's mission.

MISSION 4: THE SUPERPOWER OF SELF-LOVE

Mission 4 Activated
Open the LTUVG App and access Mission 4:
The Superpower of Self-Love

Again, congratulations on beginning this amazing journey with vulnerability and self-love. I truly mean it when I say this one exercise will transform your life in many beautiful ways, the most important being that you will be able to see why you love yourself. The work of Dr. Hawkins and his *Map of Consciousness* is something that you can reference quickly in the app so you can get a visual of how positive and negative emotions can accelerate or hamper your daily XP earned. Whenever you feel you are in a negatively charged emotion, try to listen to some music that helps you process these emotions and move into a positively charged emotion. Whenever I need to channel chaotic emotions into purpose, I put on the theme music from Gladiator or some afro beats if I need to mellow out, it works like a charm. Re-listening to your "I Love You" statements as well to transmute any subconscious emotions draining your energy field.

For added motivation, remember that every negative thought lingering in your conscious or subconscious is like a debuff drastically slowing down your leveling up progress. This keeps you from rescuing your inner child and living a happy life. Conversely, every time you say something positive about yourself, you are giving yourself a powerup to earn massively more XP and level up your ability to access the subtle energy realm.

In this next quest, we are upleveling a new skill tree, intuition. The ability to communicate with this realm of possibilities, so you, too, can see there is no spoon.

QUEST 5 - UNLOCKING OUR INTUITION

Congratulations! Your bravery and courage to try to accept yourself more and more, one day at a time, has rewarded you with an ability to see without seeing, to hear without ears, to feel without touching. What is this magical power? It's your intuition.

What is intuition? It's the ability to receive messages from the subtle energy realm communicated through the physical senses in our body (vision, feeling, hearing, taste, and smell). There are actually three other senses, but that is not our focus right now...

An example of an intuitive sense is being a clairvoyant, which means that you can send and receive messages from the subtle energy realm through vision. There is also clairsentient, intuition through feeling, clairaudience, intuition through hearing, clairalience, intuition through smelling, clairgustance, intuition through tasting, and claircognizance, intuition through an inner knowing.

Think of intuition as our ability to turn on the Heads-Up Display (HUD) for our life. You might be having a conversation with someone who seems cheerful, but if your intuition shows you the subtitle of the situation as, "this person is feeling anxious beneath their smile," you can immediately understand the deeper emotions at play and respond with more empathy.

For many of you, intuition is probably a foreign feeling that you sometimes trust, and other times are unsure of. Oftentimes we assume we're on the path to reach our goals, but what if you had the ability to pause the game, enter HUD mode, and see the fastest pathway to your desired destination? Wouldn't that be a much easier way to navigate life?

This exercise helps you hone into how your intuition communicates with you. We will practice it in low-risk situations, so that you can hear, feel, or sense your intuition easier. With practice, you will be able to pull up your HUD in the heat of battle and get cues from your intuition on the fly.

Before we jump into this, I want to share a story of an ancient people, still in existence today, who live their lives fully tuned into their intuition. They use it to communicate with Mother Earth to guide their tribe. As evidence of their ability to survive solely communicating in the subtle energy realm, they are one of the only indigenous tribes in the world to still exist outside of modernity, thriving in the Sierra Nevada de Santa Marta mountains, nearly 18,000 feet above sea level.[23] Their

---

[23] Reichel-Dolmatoff, G. (1976). Training for the Priesthood among the Kogi of Colombia. In J. Wilbert (Ed.), Enculturation in Latin America: An Anthology (pp. 265-288). UCLA Latin American Center Publications.

elders, the Mamas, are taken at birth to live in a cave for the first nine years of their lives, to learn how to trust their subtle energy senses and communicate and attune with Aluna, or Mother Earth.[24] The cave represents the womb, and the Mamas gain an intuitive connection with Pachamama (Mother Earth).

"The Mamas are masters of telepathy, with a direct link to supernatural powers in the spirit world."[25]

Why does spending time in a cave at birth assist in building intuitive powers? A hypothesis is that much like Jedi training, when we don't use our other five senses, it forces us to use our intuitive gifts to interact with our world.

Did you know that before the brain is developed, there is a heart "brain" that forms inside your mother's womb? Yep. The heart beats before the brain forms, and there is a bundle of 40,000 neurons that exist in your own heart that can process, learn, and remember. Studies by Drs. Schwaber and Vadigepalli have confirmed the existence of the "little brain" in the hearts of rats with a 3D imager, showing its placement near the sinoatrial node, which implies its use to monitor and regulate heartbeats.

We spoke previously about heart coherence, which can improve our ability to control ourselves in life. We see

---

[24] Ereira, A. (1992). The Elder Brothers: A Lost South American People and Their Wisdom. Knopf.

[25] Blaser, M. (2010). Storytelling Globalization from the Chaco and Beyond. Duke University Press.

the connection between a balanced heart rate variability, a coherent state, and enhanced communication with the little brain in our heart.

Enhancing communication is evident from studies in neurocardiology by Dr. Andrew Armour, who has demonstrated that the heart's little brain can process information, learn, remember, and even make decisions independently of the brain. Experiments show that the heart's nervous system shows characteristics associated with the neural plasticity of the brain.[26] All of this can be done without the use of sight, feeling, or touch, as this brain is solely connected to the heart, developed in the womb. I would hypothesize that the neurons in the hearts of the Mamas are even more developed than ours.

They came down from the mountains in the '90s, learned Spanish, and connected with the BBC to share the message that "civilized humans" were destroying the earth, and to change our ways, lest we destroy us all. If this topic interests you, I highly recommend watching the documentary *From the Heart of the World: The Elder Brother's Warning* to get inspiration on what you might tap into if you practice building up your intuition.

Time to practice! I'm excited for you. Today when you practice, go somewhere quiet where you can ground yourself.

For consistency, I recommend creating a space in your home or room where you have some incense or palo

---

[26] Armour, J. A. (1991). "Anatomy and function of the intrathoracic neurons regulating the mammalian heart." *The Anatomical Record*, 229(2), 482-492.

santo, ethically sourced preferably, to clear energy and do these exercises. We'll cover why these tools are valuable in a bit. Think of it as your "Gaming Sanctuary" for practicing your new and evolving "life skills." The intention of setting up your space is a great way to clear out any distracting thoughts for these exercises. Remember, we have 60,000 thoughts a day! In order to clear up these thoughts so we can receive the intuitive thoughts, we need to cleanse them first. Eventually you reach a level where you can activate your HUD by counting from three to one, but we have to start at ground zero to build up to that point. Just like building good habits, developing good practices in the beginning will allow us to eventually be masters of tapping into our intuition.

Even if it's at the same desk you work or study, find some ethically sourced sage/palo santo, a candle, and put it with your journal as your "Game of Life" kit. It will be cheaper than any gaming system you've ever purchased, I promise. I have a "Medicine Bag" or Satchel that I carry with me wherever I go. It's invaluable.

MISSION 5: INTUITION'S DETECTOR TEST

Unlike the Mamas of the Kogi, you are remembering how to tap into your natural intuition after decades (or more) relying on the five physical senses. In this moment, forget about these material senses. The senses that connect you to the physical realm. For it is in that moment of forgetting that you will remember how to connect with so much more.

It's important to be patient with yourself as you slowly activate your intuition to create consistent environments where you can settle your thoughts, such that your analytical mind isn't overactive.

Did you Know? There is an inverse relationship between our analytical mind and our intuition. When our analytical mind is active, clear messages from our intuition get blocked out. It's like trying to listen to classical music while 80's are blasting, the inspiring frequencies get drowned out by the louder vibrations. Trust that as you practice calming thoughts, intuition will start to naturally shine through. That's also a misconception, that to receive messages from our intuition, we need to DO something. The truth is to receive messages from your intuition, you enter a moment of doing NOTHING.

When we quiet our thoughts, breathe coherently, and observe our body, particularly our heart, we get a sense of how we are feeling. This is entering a state of BEING.

To be human, is to care for one another.

This next quest will also facilitate an improvement in your trust in your intuitive connection with your inner knowing.

So, without further ado, let's activate your intuition and jump into the LTUVG app to unlock the Intuition's Detector Test.

Mission 5 Activated
Open the LTUVG App and access Mission 5:
Intuition's Detector Test

How are you feeling after this mission? I'll let you in on a secret, this exercise was one of the most difficult for me. I felt unsure, awkward, but still curious. This exercise came from a very high-level teacher of mine.

When I learned it, I was unsure exactly how my intuition communicated with me. I wanted to be clairvoyant, but my wife's visions were like a movie compared to my clips of information. Consequently, this drill made me a bit self-conscious. What if my voice only speaks to me and I don't see any visions? How did I surrender to this feeling? I reminded myself that it wasn't about me doing anything, it was and is simply about me being.

The best thing to do if you feel apprehensive about this exercise is to open your heart and accept that you're going to look and feel silly. And whatever is supposed to happen will happen regardless of whether you worry about it or not. Get out of the head and move into the heart.

Lean into that silliness and watch how it might surprise you with some clear messages from your inner self. A part of your inner child that you are on a journey to rescue.

Keep on trying, and observe what felt positive, and what felt negative, with no judgment. We'll see you tomorrow for a method to help guide your intuition if you truly are struggling with a decision.

QUEST 6 - SERVICE TO OTHERS EMPOWERS OURSELVES

Vulnerability opens our heart, which acts as the core muscle for activating our intuition. This connection enhances our ability to receive guidance from our inner knowing through the subtle energy realm. Think of inner knowing as our confidence in our ability to communicate through the subtle energy realm with our higher self. It takes practice and confirmation through trial and error. To further support this process, we can lean into Service to Others, our next essential V.I.S.A. attribute.

By focusing on serving the greater good, we foster a deeper connection with others, amplifying our compassionate engagement with our world. When we help others, it creates the opportunity to realize and be grateful for what we do have, instead of focusing on the pain of what we don't have. We also subdue our analytical mind from rationalizing because another choice is more practical. For example, choosing to volunteer for a cause you believe in when you're in pain instead of drowning the pain in self-destruction. Or choosing to work for a company you believe in vs taking the job you hate that pays more money.

This holistic approach of being in service to others not only enriches our own lives but also positively impacts those around us, creating a ripple effect of healing and transformation.

To understand this a bit more, let's start with a gaming analogy this time to keep things fresh, and then support it with impactful real-world examples.

In any given RPG, building out a party always involves a healer. Someone who solely focuses on healing and buffing up other characters. That may even be the role you play in games, and it makes you feel good to see others succeed, and the party accomplishes its objective.

Remember that connection to the subtle energy realm is what builds our mana? Our ability to cast magic spells? If a healer can increase the health, give buffs like haste, and improve unique attributes, then they are technically expanding those characters' connection with the magical realm. This becomes a positive feedback loop when all party members are aligned to a cause, the healers are healing and buffing, the DPS (damage per second) machines are dealing with damage, and the tanks are taking damage for the team. Everyone in the group seems to thrive.

I know what you're thinking. I thought this once as well.

"If helping others helps ourselves, where are the real-world examples to support this theory?"

Fortunately, this incredible true story I'm about to share will illuminate several small, and large-scale examples of the power of positive intention. Specifically communal positive intention.

There was a journalist, Lynne McTaggart, who had heard of the power of intention, the ability to effect change in the physical world, simply with thoughts. During a large conference, she decided to try an experiment to assess this theory. She was presenting in Australia and had asked her audience to send the "intention of growth" to her seedlings (plants) in the United States. What she found was that the plants, during that exact moment in time, showed significant improvements in growth compared to the control plants that did not receive these intentions. Bananas!

Astounded, Lynne took this experiment a step further and tried it by attempting to create localized peace. She named this the Peace Intention Experiment[27]. For multiple days in the middle of September 2008, participants from around the world sent positive intentions of peace to the Wanni area of Sri Lanka. Coincidentally, it was during that same time that the Sri Lankan government made significant inroads in battles against the rebels in that area, eventually reducing death tolls, and leading to an eventual end to the twenty-six-year war in May of 2009. Coincidence? Who knows? I'd like to believe that there truly is the power of intention. Lynne's curiosity wanted to believe as well. Her main curiosity, however, wasn't on the incredible healing "miracles" that were happening. While they were amazing, McTaggart's focus was on the healing effects the 8 participants experienced in their own lives. These

---

[27] https://lynnemctaggart.com/the-peace-intention-experiment/

results were eventually published in her book, *The Power of Eight*.

Lynne found that between 38-44 percent of participants experienced transformations and healing in their lives as well as their relationships with family and spouses. Fascinated by what Lynne referred to as the "rebound effect," McTaggart distilled her experiments down into groups of eight people. She had a group of "healers" come together for months at a time to send healing to a given target or "healee." There were countless examples of transformative healing, but the most remarkable one was of a Wes Chapman, who had stage 4 metastatic cancer[28]. With only a few months to live, Wes had heard of these intention experiments and asked to be the subject of the healing intentions of these groups. Lynne obliged, and after multiple sessions, not only did Wes' cancer stop growing, but it receded until he fully healed! A full-blown miracle.

Now what about the healers? What type of "miracles" did they experience? Of the many, one woman, who had been suffering from migraines for years, reported that her headaches disappeared completely, while another man suffering from chronic depression reported a profound shift in his emotional state, feeling a renewed sense of purpose and human connection.

Just as in your RPG parties, when intentions are aligned, giving to others with pure intentions benefits the entire party. How do we apply this in our lives, in a practical

---

[28] McTaggart, Lynne. "The Power of Eight: Harnessing the Miraculous Energies of a Small Group to Heal Others, Your Life, and the World." Atria Books, 2017.

sense? I'm not asking you to go find a group of friends and send healing thoughts to people you care about or need healing. You could, if you were an overachiever, but it's certainly not a requirement. To simplify things, Service to Others acts as a barometer of which pathway to take when working through challenging moments in life.

Spend time every day asking, how can I help those around me prosper? You will find that others will want to help you prosper in kind. This is what my wife and I did in the heart of COVID. We dove into studying energy healing, sound healing, breathwork, and through the miraculous healings we've helped others receive, we have received the blessing of funding to open our own retreat space (Amaroo) in the cloud forest of Ecuador. We'll go into more detail on this magical piece of paradise later in this book, but for the time being, just know that everything I ask of you, we live every day. We used our intuition to guide us on this path, tapping into all the gifts that are awakening within you.

If you are building your intuition and are at a crossroads, asking "Do I go left or do I go right?", consider what is best for the group vs. what is best for you. Maybe try something different and do it for others, to see where that guides you. Take the pathway that serves the whole and observe your intuitive messages along the way. To practice this new skill in a safe environment, let's sit with today's ancient practice. Head to the LTUVG app and hop into today's mission.

MISSION 6: TONGLEN FOR TRANSFORMATION

Mission 6 Activated

Open the LTUVG App and access Mission 6: *Tonglen for Transformation*

You can initiate this ancient practice of Tonglen in meditation or during everyday activity whenever it comes to mind. As you improve at this practice, awareness of the bidirectional call and receipt of the subtle energy field around you expands. You feel the connection between people who you are not physically touching, taking in their pain, and sending them energy and expanding this to the greater whole, your energy field will begin to intuitively understand that we are all one. We utilize this practice before unlocking our last Universal Attribute.

If you are feeling a bit exhausted, please take a day or two and practice these new skills. As you level up there will be growth periods where you'll need to take space for yourself. Remember that with great power requires great vulnerability. So, give yourself the grace to absorb these new abilities with time. When you're ready, come back, I'll be right here.

QUEST 7 - RAISING OUR AWARENESS

When you think about awareness as an attribute in life, what do you think of? Someone who can see the bigger picture in any situation? When I think of heightened awareness, they are usually the people who are calm under pressure and don't get flustered by chaos because they see how to get from point A through the drama of B and C, to the destination. Having a heightened awareness is essentially being fully present. For anyone who saw Michael Jordan play basketball, he was well known for making clutch plays to win games in the final seconds. It's been said,

"That Jordan's greatest superpower wasn't his athleticism; it was his ultimate presence."

In any given challenge, he knew what actions were needed to accomplish his goal of winning a championship. This isn't to take away from his work ethic, his resilience, or his natural-born gifts. There are many who have his stature and work ethic but never touched his dominance. It's because in those clutch moments where the fate of the game is on the line, MJ's awareness and will to win was the greatest in the room.

Now there aren't many of us who can "be like Mike" and just turn on awareness like a superpower. But how would you like a different superpower? The ability to slow down time, similar to "Bullet Time" in *Max Payne*? I call it entering "Elevated States of Consciousness," by hitting the ESC button. Much like pausing a game, entering ESC allows you to become the observer of your experience, seeing the forest from the trees. It's like seeing yourself in the movie of your life, but from the perspective of the audience. When we watch a movie, we can usually tell what the protagonist should be doing, or at least, what not to do. "Don't go upstairs!", or "Don't open the door!" for example.

But what if we could see our life situation from a bird's eye view on command and receive guidance on what to say, or not to say, in many of life's challenging moments? That's what hitting the ESC button in life can do. But how? How do we enter Elevated States of Consciousness? By tuning our brain to different frequencies.

Did you know: the brain can function much like a radio? Tuning to different channels to send and receive information on various wavelengths? When you sleep, your brain slows down and the frequency of waves it emits are called delta waves. When you wake up, your brain slowly speeds up to produce beta waves, which are the frequencies we operate on every day. In between those, in descending order, we have alpha and theta waves. Both are slower than beta brain waves, and because of this, if we enter states of consciousness that operate on these wavelengths, we can observe life from a higher point of view. Delta - sleep, Theta - deep meditation/journeying, Alpha - flow state, Beta - material realm interaction, Gamma - transcendent/mystical experiences.

Think of it as switching game modes—when in active mission mode, you're in a beta state, moving through your daily challenges. What happens if you encounter a challenge where you become triggered and angry? Then you're typically entering what's called "high beta" brainwave mode, also known as FoF. Energy is being used inefficiently, but intensely, and draining us of presence.

Instead, if you hit the ESC button, drop into a state of calm, or alpha mode, then you see that this obstacle is just a challenge in life to overcome. The emotion of anger, for example, is just a goomba from Mario. To defeat it, you just jump over it and that emotion won't attach to you.

Remember, every day you have a finite number of experience points that you can gain to level up your attributes, and if you let these moments pass by, especially the triggering state ones, you want to enter Major Payne's "Bullet Time" mode. The only way to do this is by hitting the ESC button.

MISSION 7: AWARENESS IN EVERYTHING

How do we enter Elevated States of Consciousness? It's simple, but not easy. The theme continues. It's something that yogis and meditators have written thousands of books about, but you have a leg up on all of them, because you have gaming as a reference and me as your guide. This is the moment when you finally get the last laugh on people who said, "gaming is a waste of time."

You might have guessed it, but the way to enter ESC is by meditating. If you haven't meditated before, starting might seem daunting, and there is a misconception that you must "empty your mind" to successfully meditate.

Since most of us have 60,000 thoughts, and 70% of them negative, when we sit to meditate, it's difficult to clear all these thoughts out. It's especially difficult when you hear "this is dumb," "I can't meditate," "I should be doing something better with my time." Fortunately, I'm not a proponent of that type of meditation, and neither are my teachers. It doesn't mean that there aren't times when I do spring cleaning with my thoughts, but by and large:

The essence of meditation is simply to be in the present moment.

You can be running, walking, eating, writing, sitting silently, playing a sport or a musical instrument. It takes focus and intentionality, but a good starting point with the feeling of meditating is to find something that you do with undeniable presence. It could even be gaming, whether it's in a First Person Shooter or competitive match of *Super Smash Bros*. The important part is that you have a connection doing something in life, where you are actively focusing on one thing. All worry and stress melts away and you are just there, and it feels natural.

Jump into the LTUVG app and I'll show you how.

Mission 7 Activated

Open the LTUVG App and access Mission 7: *Awareness in Everything Meditation*

Welcome back life gamer, how did you enjoy that meditation? Quite different I'm sure than anything you've done before. The great spiritual teacher Osho, who designed the meditation we just did, gives a definition of meditation that I love, and that is:

"Meditation is not an activity; it is an attitude."

It is the attitude of being in the present moment. We practice meditation in calm moments, so that when we are in moments that trigger us, we can enter "Bullet Time" so we can woosah and not lose our temper. We practice meditation in moments of calm so we can hit the ESC button and become the observer of our experience at any moment. So that we can understand why it is happening. Remember, the more difficult moments in our life will net us the most XP.

Challenges aren't happening to us,
They are happening for us, to learn
from, and level up.

SAVE POINT 1 - SKILL ASSESSMENT

Congratulations! You've made it to your first major "save point." Yes, you know what that means. Yup, your first major boss battle is coming up! It will test the skills and abilities you've activated thus far, but before we do, let me ask, do you see how your Vulnerability, Intuition, Service to Others, and Awareness all work together? If you're still sitting with this question, that's perfectly normal. This is a lot of information, and it took me a lot of time to see how they supported one another. So, let's go through them together.

1. Vulnerability: Opens the door to being honest with ourselves and allows us to be our authentic self in any situation. It also allows us to forgive ourselves when we fall short of this expectation. Before we can say I am happy, we must authentically say I.

Our authentic self unlocks the I.

2. Intuition: Unlocking our intuition allows us to communicate with our higher self through our inner knowing, guiding our spirit avatar in the game of life. This connection happens in the subtle energy realm and manifests uniquely for everyone. Practicing communicating with our higher self with vulnerability refines and strengthens our intuitive abilities.
3. Service to Others: Helps to validate our intuition. When we are attempting to decipher the difference between a positive impulse vs. a negative or neutral impulse from our intuition feels like, making a choice for the greater good can be a hint in the best choice for the good of all. When we see the benefits of listening to that impulse, we associate that impulse with affirmative intuition. Remember:

Do not confuse "service to others" with "sacrificing yourself."

The Tonglen meditation, which involves taking in others' pain and sending out love, enhances our understanding of service and connects us with others through the subtle energy realm.

4. Awareness: Daily practices of connection with intuition expand our awareness, allowing us to be present and access Elevated States of Consciousness easier. Being an observer in our reality connects us to the subtle energy realm, allowing us to earn more XP from each challenge. As we earn more XP, so does our V.I.S.A.'s potential.

We've just scratched the surface on the abilities that our Universal Attributes will unlock. As you level each one up, I've devised a Universal Attribute Skill Assessment.

Let's see how far you've upgraded your passport to the subtle energy realm. Take this ten-to-fifteen-minute assessment, and it will give you a good sense of how much you've expanded in just this short amount of time.

This is going to feel a little more like a quiz, with about twenty scenarios per attribute that you can assess yourself with. You can take one attribute at a time, so there is no need to do all four categories in one sitting if you don't have the time. The importance again, is to be honest with yourself. You're the only one who suffers if you are not.

These are not theoretical scenarios that you can fudge the answers on. They're questions on how you have actually responded in life. If you have not done these things in their fullness, then the answer is no.

For example, Zai'Ra and I just finished completing our first vision quest, where we spent five days and four nights in the wilderness atop the Andes Mountains where our only shelter was a tree, a wool blanket, and the clothes on our back.

We were alone, each of us "planted" at different trees protected by a fence of 365 prayers that we tied into red cloth with tobacco and connected with red yarn. A vision quest is a rite of passage for shamans walking the path to be healing practitioners. It is a dedication to the people whom we want to find healing; to humanity, so it can awaken and protect Mother Earth; and to the Universe. While Zai'Ra and I believed we could complete a vision quest, I could not check that off my "Service to Others" Assessment until we were "harvested" and came down that mountain. Don't worry, this will not be on your checklist, but one day, who knows, maybe you will get this upgrade to your V.I.S.A.

Let's see where you are! Head into the LTUVG app and open the Save Point 1 mission where you'll find the V.I.S.A. Skill Assessment and start with the Vulnerability skill. Next, continue through the other three skill trees to see how much you've progressed so far!

! Save Point 1: !

Skill Assessment Unlocked
Go to LTUVG App

BOSS QUEST 1 – FORGIVENESS FREES YOU

Wow, just wow. You have attempted some pretty difficult internal work that most people don't have the courage to do in a lifetime, and you are still coming back for more! For anyone who played *God of War*, the most recent adaptation is very similar to the journey we are on, although with less blood and gore.

We are on a journey to heal a part of ourselves that has been hidden from us for years, probably decades. It's our inner child. In the case of Kratos, who had a long past of fighting and killing anything in the way of getting his revenge against the gods, he now was a father. With a son who he wanted to raise in a different way, to atone for his past. By the same token, without these experiences, he wouldn't be where he was, or who he was. He wouldn't have his son, nor have the skills to protect the people he loved along the way. On this journey he learns to accept who he is while also learning to trust and accept his son. In doing so, he accepts and forgives himself. Trusting that he can control his inner rage, Kratos harnesses it to change his world for the better. Whereas previously, he had left a pathway of destruction in his wake, Kratos now realizes that he can conquer his demons while keeping the people he cares about safe.

A real-life example of this is my dear father, who grew up in South Central LA during the riots, as an African American man. He experienced friends being killed, family members dying tragically, the danger of gangs, and had his life threatened by the LAPD. Despite the racism, bigotry, and gang violence around him, he never drank, never smoked, and chose to leave LA to play football in Washington State, where he met my mom. He found love, he found peace, and he built a family.

They were living the American dream: a house with a picket fence, three beautiful kids, a dog, a pool, and stable jobs as a teacher and nurse. He thought he had escaped his past, until one day, chaos unraveled it all. His marriage fell apart due to the anger that had been bottled up inside him, he was racially targeted for sexual harassment (a case he would eventually win), and he lost the ability to see his kids consistently. You see, even though Washington was safer than being in Los Angeles, it was incredibly racist. I remember being called the N word at least three times growing up, with one of those times my mother being referred to as a N-lover. As the only African American teacher in his school district, when the divorce from my mother, who was white, became public, he saw his entire network turn against him.

The sad part was that even though my father was acquitted and the school district paid him for damages to his character and career, he never fully recovered. He never taught again as a full-time teacher. For those same newspapers that reported my dad's formal accusation on the front page, only publicized his acquittal on page ten. He had to move across the state to Seattle, five hours from his children, to try to find a new teaching job. He eventually found stability as a physical trainer and substitute teacher, but he was forever bitter toward the people who he felt had been responsible for his career's untimely demise.

My devoted father put himself through hell and back to be in our lives during that time. Driving across the state on his visitation weekends, spending money he didn't have on credit cards to put us up in hotels, so we felt like we had a stable home with him. We always used to get video games for Christmas, something that I now know was an incredible luxury. I also remember one Christmas, there was a new game that had come out that we wanted to play. My dad couldn't afford to get us gifts, let alone come to visit us, but he somehow got us a new PlayStation and *Crash Bandicoot*! I loved that platformer.

As we were opening the box frantically as kids do, I remember my dad grabbing my shoulder and saying, "Chris, we have to be careful with the packaging, in case we have to take it back." A little confused and naive as a kid would be, I asked, "Why would we need to take it back?" He cleared his throat, and said softly, "Daddy can't afford to buy these things, but he wanted to make sure you had the Christmas you asked for."

It was at that moment that I first realized the sacrifices he made for us. The hotels, the lifestyle we were still living, were all rented. My father was doing it for us and bearing all the weight of the tragedy that had happened to him through it all. I made a promise to myself that my father would never have to make a financial sacrifice for our happiness again. When my brother and I moved in with him, we studied in school, trained in football, got our own jobs, and worked tirelessly until we both got into Princeton with grants covering most of our schooling. We still had time to play lots of video games as well (the reason we got jobs).

The tragedy in all of this is that even though my brother and I used this trauma as fuel to propel us higher in life, my father still held onto the pain. This trauma then turned into more pain until it transformed into suffering. Any mention of the school, the divorce, racism, a perceived slight in the grocery store would send him into a trigger loop of anger and frustration. It tarnished his relationships and culminated in more trauma, the loss of our younger brother. While his loss is nobody's fault, we all felt the loss that shattered the home my dad fought to hold together.

After this tragedy, it was hard to come home during winter breaks in college because of the stress a small incident would create. Trips home built more stress than they alleviated. Home no longer felt safe.

This set me on another mission. A mission to heal myself of this trauma. A ten-year journey of healing led to my wife and me, many years later, opening Amaroo, the aforementioned retreat center in Ecuador. We were married there, and for our second anniversary, we invited our entire family to come celebrate with us and experience ancestral healing.

The Sacred Re-Union, as we called it, served multiple purposes. The first was to celebrate our wedding with our family! We got married when travel wasn't possible for many of our family members, and we wanted to celebrate this amazing experience with them. The second motive, to create an opportunity for our loved ones to heal from ancestral trauma. Especially my father.

After nearly thirty years of harboring all the pain of his past, my father, who was a specimen of fitness decades ago, had to be stretched just to rise out of bed in the morning. He had severe back pain, slipped discs, and a pinched sciatic nerve for the last ten years. Multiple doctors told him that he would need back surgery to even have a chance at living a normal life. Playing any kind of sport again was a dream of the past, as he had already had multiple cortisol shots to mask the pain he was in. Being in pain became my dad's modus operandi.

Where is this story going? It's about to culminate in one of the biggest miracles I have ever seen. By miracle, I mean an instantaneous cure that cannot be explained by modern science. Miracles happen every day, and when you are living with an expansive V.I.S.A., they don't just happen to other people, they'll happen to you. What was this miracle?

The only thing that has inspired my dad, even at the ripe age of seventy, to change, is his kids. He would move mountains for us, and even though he had never taken any mind-altering drugs in his life, he was willing to try anything that would help him be closer to his kids. He also wanted to finally let go of his pain.

Once in Ecuador, we organized some activities that were designed, like this book, to dive deeper into the self and included some ancient healing techniques such as: sweat lodge, breathwork, sound meditations and various types of plant medicines.

Even though he had massive back pain, my father was a full participant in everything. He even crawled into a 3-hour Temazcal or sweat lodge. Temazcal is ancient technology, a ritual where participants go inside an adobe igloo and sit for four periods of forty-five minutes while fifty-two hot lava rocks are brought in. These rocks create steam inside, turning the igloo into a sauna, where participants chant, sing, and cleanse their spirits. Each period coincides with an element and a phase of our lives. Air, birth; water, adolescence; fire, adulthood; earth, death and rebirth. After the fourth period, each participant emerges reborn.

It was in this sacred womb that my father released his pain, asked for forgiveness from his children, forgave his parents, and forgave himself. It was awe-inspiring. I'm getting tears just typing these words because what happened next was another miracle. He walked out of the Temazcal under his own power and didn't need any help walking the rest of the night! He was pain-free!

Unfortunately, this was not a permanent miracle, and this panacea from pain was short-lived. He woke up the next morning, and the pain in his back was back. Again, we had to stretch and help him out of bed. Ugh! If I'm fully honest with you, we were fighting back showing our disappointment. We did our best to have faith that if there was a chance for miraculous healing, he just needed to keep going down that pathway of forgiveness.

That evening, we signed him up for shamanic bodywork with an amazing shaman named Cesar. Shamanic bodywork is a combination of somatic breathwork, ancestral limpia (cleansing), and deep tissue massage. We are going to work a lot with somatic breathwork in this book, which is essentially breathing in a way that brings traumatic energy to the surface, so you can release it.

Did you know: your body stores unhealed trauma inside of it in the form of disruptive energy? It's quite remarkable, and the book *The Body Keeps the Score* by Van der Kolk compares traumatic energy to battle-sites within the body.[29] Think of it like a Mario-level map. Every place where you have trauma in the body that is unresolved is an open level that you need to overcome. When you overcome these levels, you receive a star, or the Gems of Understanding that you are on the hunt for. However:

As long as we suppress our trauma,
we are waging war against ourselves.

---

[29] Van der Kolk, B. (2014). The Body Keeps the Score: Brain, Mind, and Body in the Healing of Trauma. Viking.

Van der Kolk goes even further in his studies to show that even if we heal ourselves psychologically from our trauma, we still need to release the energy somatically, or from the physical form of the body. Looking back at this memory, I realized this was why my dad had to go into this bodywork session.

I remember talking to my dad before the session. I was preparing him for the pain of the session, encouraging him to breathe through it. Shamanic bodywork isn't for the weak of heart; you are breathing through the release of intense pain. But before I could get the words of caution out of my mouth, he just looked at me in the eyes and said,

"Son, I'm ready to let this go."

I get chills just thinking about the calmness and surrender in his voice. It was as if he knew what he had to do, and he was going to finally overcome this boss level in his life.

I kid you not. After my father came out of this somatic session, he was like a kid again. A super strong one. With excitement, he bent down, touched his toes, walked his hands out into a plank-position, and did three superman pushups! (YouTube that if you don't know what that is) He then walked his hands back, stood up, and looked at us with this beaming smile, saying, "No more pain! I'm healed!"

He just turned 70 this past month, and he is benching 225, deadlifting 135 lbs., playing pickleball, and still raving about the miraculous healing he received with no surgery! If you want to see this video miracle, please email me and I would be honored to share it with you if it can inspire you to embrace the same level of forgiveness my dad did. Oprah once said,

"Forgiveness is accepting the past couldn't have happened any other way."

I truly believe that. It's because every experience is meant to serve to guide you back to your true self. Without the trauma, maybe something different happens, but we are here for a purpose, and part of that purpose is remembering how to forgive. To remember to be vulnerable, as my dad was in the Temazcal; to use your intuition, as we did with giving him the shamanic bodywork session after the pain returned; to be in service to others, as the shamans were for us and our father; and to be present, as we all were, especially my father in releasing his pain in that final healing session. It was about ninety minutes of breathing and screaming, which took an immense amount of presence and courage.

As a healing practitioner, it's good practice to never say, "I healed you." If you ever work with someone who says, "I healed you," I strongly advise you to thank them for their services and never come back. You are your greatest healer. Everyone has the power to heal themselves, and as a healing practitioner, I am only a guide for your healing.

So, are you ready to heal yourself? You have the tools to do some life-shifting forgiveness, and all it takes is some breathing, your V.I.S.A., a pen and a piece of paper. So, let's navigate to the LTUVG App and find Boss Mission 1: Forgiveness Frees You, happy surrendering!

BOSS MISSION 1: FORGIVENESS FREES YOU

> **Boss Mission 1 Activated**
> Open the LTUVG App and access Boss Mission 1: *Forgiveness Frees You*

As you continue your healing process, remember that every new activity earns you more XP. Unlike a video game, we don't have a visual of how close we are to leveling up, but like a video game, as soon as you level up, the game (or life) feels better. How will this show up in real life?

A test to show when you've overcome the negative emotions associated with a person or event, when you can stop writing that person's name, is when you no longer become emotionally charged when you think about this event. That is halfway to your goal. The final challenge is when you think of that person as your teacher and find gratitude for the lesson they taught you.

For example, my parents' divorce took me to a bigger city, where I could be recruited for football and go to a prestigious university like Princeton. I think about that event with gratitude, and all of the lessons it taught me about love, commitment, and surrender to the flow of the Universe. Keep surrendering to the process of forgiveness, and you will level up tremendously.

Forgiveness isn't for the person/event that caused you pain. Forgiveness is for you.

Level 2 Recap:

- Subtle Energy Grinding Activities
  - (V) Self-love Practice
  - (I) Intuition's Detector Test
  - (S) Tonglen Meditation
  - (A) Osho Presence Meditation
- Boss Activity Unlocked
  - Forgiveness Frees You
- Universal Tools Acquired
  - V.I.S.A. Assessment

LEVEL 3

YOUNIVERSE

Congratulations! You have activated your V.I.S.A. to navigate the subtle energy realm of life! You are going to accomplish things faster, gain more experience (points) from each challenge in life, and remain calm while you move through these challenging experiences. You've learned a cheat code in life, and it will never be the same. Life is infinitely more fun when you wake up every day excited to master the game of life. When you wake up and start to see every part of your day as a level in a game, you'll realize that each challenge provides an opportunity to level up your YOUniverse. You'll hear me use this term, and it was something that I picked up from a dear teacher of mine, a student of the amazing teacher Drunvalo Melchizedek[30]. What does this mean? No, it's

[30] Melchizedek, D. (2000). The Ancient Secret of the Flower of Life, Volume 1. Light Technology Publishing.

not that the world revolves around you; but that it does happen for you, to level up.

The Hawaiian practice and way of life Ho'oponopono is based on a similar structure[31]. It suggests that we aren't eight billion people living in one world, but eight billion worlds sharing one collective consciousness. This concept aligns with the idea of your personal YOUniverse, where your experiences of the whole, are meant to teach you about your own wholeness. Every blessing and every broken heart are meant to remind you of the beautiful building blocks that make up, you.

Imagine an RPG with no enemies, no obstacles, no challenges, no "boss levels." How would you expect to level up with no mechanism to earn XP? How would you learn the capabilities of your avatar without having to navigate challenges? That's all that life's challenges are. Mirrors showing you how to become the master of your own world.

As we continue into this level, and you continue suspending disbelief, we'll touch on theories based in quantum science that support this perspective. The field of quantum mechanics has shown us that the observer plays a crucial role in shaping reality[32], lending credence to the idea that each of us might indeed be at the center of our own universe. This doesn't mean we're separate

---

[31] Vitale, J. (2007). Zero Limits: The Secret Hawaiian System for Wealth, Health, Peace, and More. John Wiley & Sons.
[32] Rosenblum, B., & Kuttner, F. (2011). Quantum Enigma: Physics Encounters Consciousness. Oxford University Press.

from others, but rather that we're all interconnected in ways we're only beginning to understand.

QUEST 8 - SCRATCHING THE SURFACE!

"Kanyini, how did you grow into your lifestyle?" you might be wondering. If you can't tell by now, I did not grow up in a spiritual family. In fact, after the tragic loss of my first sister before she reached 5 months old, my parents struggled to find connection with a God who would let their innocent daughter die. I later realized that Diana's loss wasn't solely to cause us pain, but to bring our family closer together. That took a long time to see through that pain, which also brought me more pain, and suffering.

Fast forward thirty years, and I am living a successful, but mostly unconscious life, overachieving in the financial capital of the world, New York City. I had just taken a job with a brilliant salesman from Peru, who had just taken a sabbatical to open a retreat space in Peru hosting Ayahuasca ceremonies. This was the first time I had come across "plant medicine," but it was clear that it was something that would help me. I had accumulated so much trauma in life, from close deaths in the family to a near-death experience of my own, that the idea of consuming a substance that could relieve this suffering interested me.

For those who may be curious about what Ayahuasca is, it is ancient medicine. Co-created in the Amazon with Mother Earth and the Indigenous tribes that have lived there for thousands of years. This mixture of plants is brewed into tea that cleanses the body physically, emotionally, and spiritually when taken in a sacred ritual. During these ceremonies, individuals have visions that give them a deeper understanding of their traumas and a deeper sense of meaning in their lives. These visions allow participants to let go of and heal chronic dis-eases that are bi-products of pain and suffering.

While the chance to heal my trauma with this medicine intrigued me, I had one misplaced fear. I believed that Ayahuasca provided a warp tunnel that would take me on a one-way journey through time. This portal might take me to level twenty, fifty, or one hundred. "What if mama Aya takes me to level one hundred, without having the skills to navigate the monsters that reside there?" I feared.

I later learned that she only takes you on the journey you are ready for, but at the time, I decided to grind more experience points before taking on the boss level of an ayahuasca ceremony. I dove into studying shamanism, to equip myself with the tools necessary to navigate my first ayahuasca journey.

That first journey occurred three years ago, and when I sat with mother Aya for the first time, I was grateful that I had waited. I saw clearly that life was happening for me, not to me. Life indeed was just like a video game (the language of my heart), and it was mind-blowing. As an engineer, I also needed to see proof of these truths with my own eyes. Medicine showed me unequivocal evidence of the existence of the subtle energy realm. As I journeyed deeper and deeper into the spiritual realm, I asked one question, "Please show me the pathway to be 100 percent on my highest vibrational path." I was even willing to give up my high six figure job in finance (although I hoped that I could also maintain it).

She has since guided me along one major quest line:

To demystify the magic of the subtle energy realm through the lens of video games.

This book is a navigational guide of the subtle energy realm through breathwork, meditation, and visualization. Just like the first quests, we'll layer in additional concepts that provide ways to level up your Universal Attributes, sometimes even stacking XP for multiple attributes. As a gamer, I know you love doubling up XP for different skills with one activity. That's where the phrase, "kill two birds with one stone" comes into play.

The more open you are to this process of leaning into your areas of discomfort, the faster you will establish the necessary foundation for all the skills and practices that come next.

What does this mean? It means slowly establishing practices that you do daily, starting with breathwork, meditation, and journaling. Without these three practices, your skill set won't grow effectively. Think of it as a daily mission that you get XP bonuses for doing consistently. A landmark study analyzed data from over 850,000 online game players, showing that those who spread their practice over time achieved significantly higher scores than those who compressed their practice into fewer, longer sessions.[33]

In fact, they found that spacing practice over more than 24 hours led to performance gains equivalent to about five extra practice sessions. This is why I encourage you to read one level a day, doing at most two missions, so you can integrate these new skills more effectively. By applying this principle to your daily practices, you're setting yourself up for optimal growth and performance.

Do you remember *Skyrim*? Where you can level up to 100 in every category simply by using that skill? The Game of Life works similarly, which was why Skyrim was so dope. You may be predisposed to certain skills, but for Universal Skills, you can access all of them. Everyone can be vulnerable, be of service to others, listen to their intuition, and expand their awareness to be in the present moment. Will you honor the promise you made to yourself to practice fifteen minutes a day, so that you can live a healthier, fuller life where you can abundantly live in your purpose?

There are no cheat codes to this process, you must engage consistently to get stronger, and like any video game, the rules of this game follow the same principles.

Commitment check—do you want to go back to your life you had before you opened this book? Where you are no longer the superhero in your own life? Where you button mash through life losing XP point after XP point

---

[33] Stafford, T., & Dewar, M. (2014). Tracing the trajectory of skill learning with a very large sample of online game players. Psychological Science, 25(2), 511-518.

during the hardest levels in your life? Holding onto pain from trauma that turns into suffering that you navigate through sheer willpower utilizing only your Unique Skills?

Or are you ready to step into the shoes of being the hero of your reality? The master of your domain? Able to visualize the life you want and then pull that reality to you?

My ability to facilitate healing with touch (reiki), create constructs with my mind and pull those realities to me (manifesting), and more are skills that have only come online after countless hours of healing and calling in many GOUs.

I'm thrilled and excited for you to discover yours and share them in the Community that you've activated your V.I.S.A. Our Life Gamer Guild is meant to serve many purposes, with the main one being to provide community and support during your healing activation journey. Be sure to check the app for live support. Finishing this book and all its quests will take a lot of consistency, courage, and conviction, so I'm here to support that journey.

One thing that helped me write this book was a promise I made to myself, a consequence or reward that I will give myself when I finish. Raising the stakes is one of the best ways we can ensure we accomplish our goals. You could make a promise to the community on either a positive or negative outcome if you don't finish this book in a reasonable time frame—say one to two months. At our core, we can disappoint ourselves, but we don't want to disappoint others. We also don't want to do something that either costs money or embarrasses us.

This could be paying someone in your life (mom, dad, wife, husband, best friend) $5 every day if you don't do a quest in this book or taking a vow of silence if you don't finish the book in two months. Some people, like me, are more reward driven. For me, I made myself the promise that I couldn't play the new *Final Fantasy 7 Rebirth* until I published and successfully launched the book. *FF7* is one of my favorite games ever and not being able to play it has inspired me every hour to keep on writing, editing, and creating analogies that will make this book as excitingly digestible as possible.

If you are ready to commit to this journey, go to the app, go to the "Commitment Forge" Channel within the Life Gamer Guild, and announce the date you plan on finishing, and the consequence or reward you will commit to. Also, take a moment to share one thing that you've learned so far from this book.

For example, "I commit that when I finish this book, I will reward myself with a PS5 and the new FFVII game." and "So far I've learned that healing can be fun!"

That is your assignment for the day, or if you want to continue on, let's get some extra credit in today in the next section.

THE 5 BODIES OF CONSCIOUSNESS

Suspend your disbelief for a moment, and life's synchronicities will show you the way.

I don't expect you to believe life is a super-duper complex holographic universe (yet). As we move through the book, note and pay attention to all of the happy coincidences that happen in your life. Share them in the "Gratitude Lobby" Channel if you feel inspired. Similar to if you did not know that gravity existed, this force would still keep you stuck on the ground. There are Universal rules and laws that govern this world, and if you keep reading and practicing, you'll experience them for yourself.

There is a higher consciousness that is communicating with you from outside this reality. If this is a holographic universe, where we are projections or avatars within this reality, then there would ostensibly be a controller that has the ability to guide us to our highest successful path. This is what a higher, or natural self is.

Now you might be wondering, "If this were such a high-tech holographic universe, why wouldn't the controller just guide us directly?" Great question. It is my hypothesis that this super-duper, super-super-duper, super-super-super-duper complex holographic universe needs energy to thrive. That energy source is the one thing that we will always have, our free will. This is what we contribute to energize our world.

Much like the scene in *The Matrix* where that world of machines needed the energy of each human connected to it to run, we have our free will to act and do as we please. Our higher self can only guide us by putting things in our pathway, hoping we pay attention to the signs around us. We can consciously make the choice to follow our highest path, or go down a different path, it's up to us. This doesn't mean that we cannot be manipulated or controlled, but that's for a different level of this manuscript.

How does our higher self-communicate with us? In order to understand how our higher self might communicate with us, we must go into a bit of biology and quantum medicine.

<u>Did you know:</u> Dr. Amit Goswami created a framework that there are five bodies of consciousness that determine how we interact with the world around us, and how it interacts with us? It begins with our cells and the DNA within each one.[34]

The first body of consciousness, the physical body, is made up of bones, muscles, blood and flesh. The second body of consciousness is the vital body, and this is where things get interesting. While it's the second body of consciousness, it's actually the source of the first body of consciousness. The second body is the light that holds the blueprint for our physical body. How is this possible? When we are being created in our mother's womb, we start as one tiny cell, a stem cell. Every one of our cells

---

[34] **Goswami, Amit.** *The Quantum Doctor: A Physicist's Guide to Health and Healing.* Hampton Roads Publishing, 2004

starts out in this form. Within every cell, there is a command center, called DNA, and it determines which proteins the cell produces. The type of protein produced will determine what kind of cell it will become. Will it become a part of the heart, brain, eyes, or other organs in your future body? How does DNA communicate this information to the cells? Through light, which are called biophotons.[35]

Dr. Fritz Popp discovered that we are "beings of light." That our entire body is created by billions of tiny biophotons that act as the blueprint of our physical body. The massive light network of biophotons creates a morphogenetic field around every human to maintain homeostasis so that they can survive and thrive. The residual energy that this network creates is what people refer to as an aura. This energy field can be felt, and some people have the ability to see these fields as red, green, yellow, orange, blue, purple, or white. As you level up your intuition, perhaps you'll discover that you are one of these people. Or, if you are like me, you will instead sense the aura with your feelings and intuitive sense of touch.

While these concepts may seem esoteric, they are grounded in scientific observation. As noted in scientific literature, "Ultraweak photon emission (UPE) is a general term for the phenomenon of spontaneous emission of light from biological systems in the UV, visible, and IR spectral ranges."[36] This demonstrates that

---

[35] Popp, F.A. (2003). "Biophotons - background, experimental results, theoretical approach and applications." Restor Neurol Neuroscience, 21(3-4), 153-164.

[36]

the emission of light from living organisms is a scientifically observed phenomenon, providing empirical support for the concept of biophotons while maintaining a rigorous scientific approach to their study and potential significance.

Think of your body as a giant Power Ranger or Voltron, where you have different systems that control parts of the body to ensure full capacity operations. Remember, the body is always trying to maintain equilibrium, so each of these systems is also maintaining balance in one area or system. When all of these systems are in balance, they can work together to power up Voltron and overcome challenges. There are seven energy systems, or energy centers, which exist inside the vital body, also known as chakras. To integrate and deepen the practice with the previous activities of meditation, breathwork, and especially the self-love and forgiveness exercises, we will cover each chakra so that you can be aware of which ones are balanced or out of balance.

This information may require some memorization over time, but it isn't required to deepen your practice. There will be plenty of guidance with the upcoming meditations so that you can focus on the practice and not the technical aspect. But we are nerds at heart, so let's dig into the technical aspects of our very own super-powered Voltron, our body.

REMEMBERING OUR ROOTS

The first chakra, the root chakra, is located at the base of our spine. It's referred to as the root chakra because it roots us into the ground and is related to our life's purpose and connection to family. If you have chronic back issues, you might believe it is due to being overweight or out of shape. Maybe even a back injury from childhood that never quite healed. While these may be factors, it's typically only part of the story. Most people with back issues have unresolved issues with their mother, father, or siblings.

I would go as far as to wager that if you have back problems, one or all of these are areas of weakness in your life: family, job stability, abundance, safety, or all the above. If this is the case, I'm sending you positive energy and encouragement to move through this book, because if you do the work, you'll improve your quality of life.

Why am I so confident in this?

"Every chronic physical dis-ease first starts in the emotional & spiritual realm."

In Dr. Goswami's book, *The Quantum Doctor*, it's called "downward causation." This theory suggests that consciousness, rather than physical matter, is the fundamental reality. In this view, our thoughts and emotions can directly influence our physical bodies, creating a top-down effect that can manifest as physical symptoms or illnesses.[37] This paradigm shift in understanding health and disease aligns with ancient wisdom traditions and offers a new perspective on how we approach healing.

This concept of downward causation provides a framework for understanding how unresolved emotional issues or spiritual disconnections can manifest as physical ailments. It bridges the gap between modern science and holistic healing practices, offering a more comprehensive view of human health through the lens of quantum science.

While studying for my doctorate in integrative medicine, I also encountered the work of Dr. Ryke Geerd Hamer, who proposed an unconventional theory based on his observations of cancer patients. He suggested that many illnesses, particularly cancer, might have emotional or psychological roots. His perspective aligns with the idea that we exist in this world to grow and overcome challenges, much like leveling up in a video game.

These constructs for growth date all the way back to when we lived as hunter-gatherers in nature. Back then, it was the difficulty of living in nature that provided the challenges for us to learn, but over time, through the process of building city-states, those challenges have disappeared. Hamer theorized that it was this reduction in outward environmental challenges that then became mirrored as internal challenges such as cancer, heart

---

[37] Goswami, A. (2004). *The Quantum Doctor: A Physicist's Guide to Health and Healing*. Charlottesville, VA: Hampton Roads Publishing.

attacks, and the countless autoimmune diseases that continually pop up.

Dr. Hamer's interest in this area stemmed from personal tragedy. After losing his son to a tragic incident, both he and his wife were diagnosed with cancer. This coincidence led him to explore potential connections between emotional trauma and physical illness. Alongside conventional treatments, he focused on emotional healing and reported positive outcomes for both him and his wife as they healed from the loss of their son.

Could it just be coincidence that when he had emotionally healed from the loss of his son, his cancer also went away? Dr. Hamer had to find out.

He conducted further research, proposing that emotional healing could potentially influence physical health outcomes. He suggested that unresolved emotional issues manifest as physical symptoms, an idea that resonates with some holistic healing approaches.

Dr. Hamer's findings and facilitation of helping patients heal from cancer through his research were revolutionary. Why have you never heard of him and his "cure for cancer"? Because when Dr. Hamer presented his findings to the medical board in Germany, they dismissed his tens of thousands of cases as dangerous and forced him to stop doing his research. When he refused, his license was eventually taken away. He was then arrested for continuing to give free medical advice. During the trial, a prosecutor, upon studying his findings, stated that "after more than five years, of

6500 patients with mostly 'terminal' cancer, 6000 were still alive."[38]

You can still find his research online, and while I don't recommend ignoring what Western medicine says in cases when life and death are in the balance, I would always recommend that if there is a chronic physical ailment that is causing you pain, augment whatever prescription an MD gives you with emotional healing and practicing breathwork, self-love and forgiveness. If the thought of healing emotional trauma feels difficult; that is a tell-tale sign that it is the right pathway for your healing journey. Think of it as a checkpoint indicator for your mission objective of healing yourself.

Just as the most difficult levels in video games signify the biggest rewards, so too do the most difficult challenges in life provide you with the greatest opportunities for transformation. Fortunately for you, this book will empower you with abilities to help you navigate these difficulties easier.

THE BODY KEEPS THE SCORE

Previously we discussed how the book *The Body Keeps the Score* showed that any trauma that we've experienced emotionally or spiritually is stored physically in the body. From a physiological perspective, how does this happen?

---

[38] Markolin, C. (n.d.). Biography of Dr. med. Ryke Geerd Hamer. Learning German New Medicine. Retrieved August 29, 2024, from https://learninggnm.com/documents/hamerbio.html

Without going into a full lecture, I'll give you SparkNotes.

Our body has neurotransmitters which are called neuropeptides. They are sent from the brain to different parts of our body when we have an emotional reaction to something. The type of neuropeptides that are sent are determined by whether we are perceiving the event with a positive emotion like joy or bliss, or a negative emotion such as sadness, anger, or fear.

Over time, since our brains are predicting machines, once we associate a stressful event, like a demanding boss or job loss, with an experience, like not being able to pay the bills, whenever we think about work or our next rent check, stress hormones will be sent to a part of our body. And because the body typically has to feel safe before the mind can envision a better future. Living in fear can prevent us from seeing a future where we have a great boss, with a fulfilling job, and never living paycheck to paycheck again. That is, until we overcome those fears.

Eastern medicine suggests that these neuropeptides travel to our root chakra, which is associated with family, job security, and safety. This connection between emotions and physical responses is supported by the groundbreaking work of Dr. Candace Pert, who discovered that neuropeptides and their receptors form a 'biochemical substrate of emotion,' linking our mental states with bodily responses.[39]

---

[39] Pert, C. B. (1997). Molecules of Emotion: Why You Feel the Way You Feel. Scribner.

Remember how our positive or negative emotions act as buffs or debuffs for our energy levels? Think of neuropeptides as bonuses or penalties to the severity for the buffs and debuffs your emotions are placing on you.

For example, Kobe Bryant shared a story about how he went an entire summer league of basketball without scoring a point. When he was sulking, his father, an ex-NBA player, asked him why he was upset. Kobe shared his recount of being dominated by his peers. His father looked at him and said, "Whether you score 0 points or 60 points, I'm going to love you no matter what." This inspired Kobe not only to improve at basketball, but also to become an all-time great.

In Kobe's case, his father's unconditional love functioned as a bonus die, granting him extra emotional resilience to overcome the shame of scoring zero points an entire summer. This 'love buff' effectively neutralized the potential 'shame debuff' that could have made him decide to quit playing basketball altogether! Without this parental support, a level 1 shame debuff might have been the end to a potential all-time great. Instead, armed with his father's love, Kobe had a high-level buff that not only dispelled negative emotions, but also boosted his determination and confidence.

This is how our emotional experiences, mediated by neuropeptides, can shape our responses to life's challenges. A strong foundation of positive emotions, like love and acceptance, can provide a buffer against setbacks, allowing us to bounce back faster and reach greater heights. In the game of life, cultivating these positive 'buffs' through self-love, supportive relationships and self-compassion can be as crucial as any skill or talent in achieving our goals. Let's find out how.

MISSION 8: YOU'RE GROUNDED!

How do we heal our first energy center, our root chakra? The first step is to ground yourself. No, I'm not trying to trigger memories of losing your gaming or TV privileges! We are going to connect with the ground, the earth that we walk on, and "reset" our body in the process.

There is a practice called "earthing" that reduces inflammation, stress levels, and improves sleep just by making direct physical contact with the earth's surface—dirt, stones or grass![40] In another study, subjects of the test showed faster wound healing, improved blood flow, and a modulated immune response, showing beneficial responses to autoimmune diseases![41]

How and why does this work? The science of it is complex, but to simplify, let's think of an electrical circuit. Whenever you plug a large appliance into the wall, it has three prongs, with the third prong being the ground. These circuits need a ground to remain stable,

---

[40] Chevalier, G., Sinatra, S. T., Oschman, J. L., Delany, R. M. (2012). Earthing: Health Implications of Reconnecting the Human Body to the Earth's Surface Electrons. *Journal of Environmental and Public Health*. doi:10.1155/2012/291541.

[41] Oschman, J. L., Chevalier, G., & Brown, R. (2015). The Effects of Grounding (Earthing) on Inflammation, the Immune Response, Wound Healing, and Prevention and Treatment of Chronic Inflammatory and Autoimmune Diseases. *Journal of Inflammation Research*, 8, 83-96. doi:10.2147/JIR.S69656.

allowing stray voltage or energy to flow safely. The grounding wire provides a "path of least resistance" for energy discharge, preventing it from building up over time and potentially exploding through other parts of the circuit.

When you are ready for today's mission, if you can go outside for a field trip, grab your phone, and go to today's mission in the LTUVG app, and let's venture out into nature!

Mission 8a Activated
Open the LTUVG App and access Mission 8a:
Earthing for Earthlings

If you are in a city where going outside is difficult or it's too hot or cold outside, how are you supposed to ground yourself? We can connect to the earth through guided meditation and visualization. Before the mind says impossible, remember, we are "suspending disbelief" so that we can expand the limitations our mind has put on our reality.

To support this new way of thinking, here is a study conducted by the Cleveland Clinic Foundation where participants were asked to imagine strengthening their fingers and bicep while they were immobilized[42]. After three months of these mental exercises, fifteen minutes five days a week, the group found a 35 percent increase

[42] Clark, B.C., Mahato, N.K., Nakazawa, M., Law, T.D., & Thomas, J.S. (2014). The power of the mind: the cortex as a critical determinant of muscle strength/weakness. *Journal of Neurophysiology*, 112(12), 3219-3226. doi:10.1152/jn.00386.2014

in finger strength and 13.5 percent in bicep strength! If you have a gym membership and are looking to save money, cancel and just do this instead (kidding). That being said, if visualizing working out can increase muscle mass, visualizing being on the earth and connecting with Mother Earth will also have healing effects.

So go to the LTUVG app and unlock your next mission, the Grounding Grounds Me Meditation.

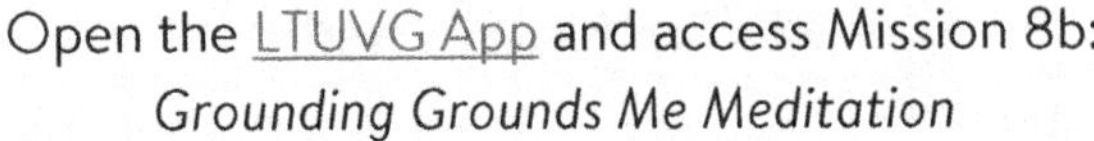

Mission 8b Activated

Open the LTUVG App and access Mission 8b:
Grounding Grounds Me Meditation

Amazing work! You now have a tool that you can do any time of the day, regardless of the weather. If you are about to have a big conversation or presentation and are nervous, open the app and go to this meditation. I have used this meditation in many of my finance meetings where a lot of money was on the line, and it's resulted in hundreds of thousands of dollars coming my way. Even when I asked the partners of my firm to promote me to Spiritual Managing Director! Yes, I got the promotion.

With repetition, you will be able to close your eyes, take a couple of Co-breaths, feel your root chakra drop into the earth, and the grounded connection of the earth in your heart. We start many of our future practices with grounding so you will feel less overwhelmed with these new concepts.

QUEST 9 - COMPLETING THE CIRCUIT

What's next? The other six energy centers! We spend more time on the first chakra because it is your foundation, and if it isn't centered, then it's like trying to build a Jenga tower standing on one block—it's unstable. And you want to be a fully stable Voltron so you can overcome any challenge life throws at you with full power.

I once heard this story about how the energy centers were connected and how they relate to one another. It really helped me understand why each one matters and also how to give them attention and care. Here it is:

Chakra (they/them) was a special tree growing in an enchanted forest. He had a grand mission to fulfill but needed to mature to discover it.

In the first year of its growth, Chakra only grew downwards. It developed strong roots that dug deep into the ground. These roots provided security and stability, absorbing nutrients from the earth. This is like our Root Energy Center (*Muladhara*), red in color, located at the base of the spine, which represents safety, stability and security, in particular with family and jobs.

In the second year, when Chakra's head popped out of the sacred earth, they immediately felt gratitude for creation. They started to become aware of their world, and possibly the reason for their existence, to flourish! This is similar to our Sacral Energy Center (*Svadhisthana*), orange in color, located below our naval, which represents creativity, connection to purpose, and sexual energies.

By the third year, the warm yellow sun shone down on Chakra, boosting its confidence as it stretched even farther into the sky. This represents our Solar Plexus Energy Center (*Manipura*), yellow in color, located just below the chest, which represents self-esteem, confidence, will-power and personal responsibility.

In the fourth year, Chakra had grown so tall that it needed to open up its branches. It opened its heart, and many limbs began to grow from its trunk. This is like our Heart Energy Center (*Anahata*), located in the center of the chest next to the heart, green in color, which represents unconditional love and connection with others.

By the fifth year, with strong roots, inspired creation, determined purpose, and an open heart, Chakra's leaves began to bloom with beautiful flowers. Birds made homes in their branches, and they sang with joy. This represents our Throat Energy Center (*Vissudha*), sky blue in color, located in the center of the throat, which represents the ability to express ourselves and communicate with others clearly.

In the sixth year, as Chakra felt safe, creative, full of confidence and gratitude from being able to express its joy through the songs of the birds, it finally noticed the other trees around it. It developed an extra sense of awareness of the larger trees that had shielded them from too much sun as well as the smaller trees and animals that thrived under their own branches. This is like our Third Eye Energy Center *(Ajna)*, indigo in color, located in the center of the forehead, which represents our intuition, foresight, and ability to connect with the subtle energy realm. It is driven by imagination.

Finally, in the seventh year, Chakra heard an internal voice, whispering for them to give more. "Give more?" they questioned...and then they realized that they both extended from their roots, and their branches. That they could share nutrients from the sky into the earth, just as they shared the fruits of their roots, from their branches. Chakra began to intuitively send nutrients through its roots to support other trees and soon became connected to the massive network of the enchanted forest. It realized it was never one tree; it was always connected to everything all at once.

Instantly, a crown of violet flowers grew atop Chakra, representing their ascension to consciousness. This represents our Crown Energy Center *(Sahasrara)*, violet in color, located in the center of the head, which represents states of higher consciousness and connects us to the Universe.

This is the allegorical story of Chakra and how its stages of growth connect with our own chakras and their subsequent meaning.

So that's it! The seven energy centers/chakras of your body and how they all function to support your body. These all make up your second body of consciousness.

Let the story of Chakra the Tree remind you of how your own energy centers are connected. Why is this important? Because if one of your chakras are out of balance, whether we have resistance to expressing ourselves in public, or prefer isolation and feeling lonely, we can use a tool to cleanse the energy of that chakra and return to balance. It's amazing, it's like being able to call on the warmth of the sun anytime, anywhere.

This is a high-level skill you'll learn later. In the next mission, I'm going to teach you how to visualize a construct that will eventually be upgraded for the purpose of chakra cleansing.

But first, we must complete the circuit covering the other bodies of consciousness, and then talk about the elephant in the room, the holographic universe theory.

ADDITIONAL LEVELS OF CONSCIOUSNESS

The third body of consciousness is the mental body; the realm of thoughts. The other two bodies we will cover in the next books, yes Life: The Ultimate Video Game is a series of manuscripts. Life is incredibly complex! There's no way I was covering everything in one book, this inspiration manual serves as the foundation for understanding these concepts so we can build on them later.

The fourth body of consciousness is the supramental body, the realm of the archetypes. If you are familiar with Carl Jung's work on archetypes[43], this realm contains universal patterns and images derived from the

---

[43] Jung, C. G. (1969). The archetypes and the collective unconscious (2nd ed.). Princeton University Press.

collective unconscious, representing fundamental human motifs[44]. Common archetypes include the Hero, the Fool, the Great Mother, and the Magician. This body of consciousness represents where we embody and interact with these universal patterns, influencing our personal growth and our role in the collective human experience.

The fifth body of consciousness is the bliss body. In essence, it is that direct connection with our divine self, our higher self, that then leads us to being connected with the whole of the Universe. Imagine being everywhere and nowhere all at once, with an infinite source of energy emanating from your core. This is just a fraction of what it feels like.

Why are these five bodies of consciousness important and what the heck does it have to do with being in a holographic universe?

Think about any video game, from the simplest Atari game to the most complex MMORPG on PS5. Everything in the game comes from the CPU. Every aspect of the game is programmed, from the main characters to the blades of grass, to the wind blowing them randomly while you play. If we existed in a holographic universe, a super-duper complex video game, then there would have to be systems that would allow us to interact with this reality. A hypothesis is that the five bodies of consciousness are how we

---

[44] Stevens, A. (2006). The archetypes. In R. K. Papadopoulos (Ed.), The handbook of Jungian psychology: Theory, practice and applications (pp. 74-93). Routledge.

communicate with the Universe around and inside us, and how it communicates with us.

THE ELEPHANT IN THE ROOM - HOLOGRAPHIC UNIVERSE THEORY

What scientific evidence supports the theory of a holographic universe, and how does it relate to the concept of a higher self, or natural self? I'll leave the ultimate judgment to this concept until the end, but to start, let's consider the work of David Bohm, a renowned physicist whom Einstein greatly respected and once referred to as his "spiritual son."[45] Bohm, who the Dalai Lama referred to as his "science guru," made substantial contributions to quantum physics and developed intriguing ideas about the nature of reality.

Bohm's work at Berkeley contributed to the Manhattan Project, although he was unable to obtain clearance to work directly with the project. His subsequent research significantly advanced quantum theory, particularly through his interpretation of quantum mechanics and his theory of the "implicate order"[46]. Bohm proposed that the tangible reality of our everyday lives might be analogous to a holographic image, suggesting a deeper, underlying order to the universe.

The concept of a holographic universe posits that, like a hologram, the universe might encode information about the whole in each of its parts. This idea finds some

---

[45] Peat, F. D. (1997). Infinite Potential: The Life and Times of David Bohm. Basic Books.

[46] Bohm, D. (1980). Wholeness and the Implicate Order. Routledge.

parallel in how holograms are formed. A hologram is created when coherent light, typically from a laser, is split and then recombined to create an interference pattern. This pattern, when illuminated properly, produces a three-dimensional image in what is referred to as a "hologram."[47]

What exactly is a hologram? Remember the scene from *Star Wars*, when Princess Leia recorded a holographic message to Obi-Wan? That is a hologram, a projection of a 2D image into the 3D as if it's real, but it's an illusion. To help visualize this a bit better, I'm going to show you our first diagram, which will help this process out a ton!

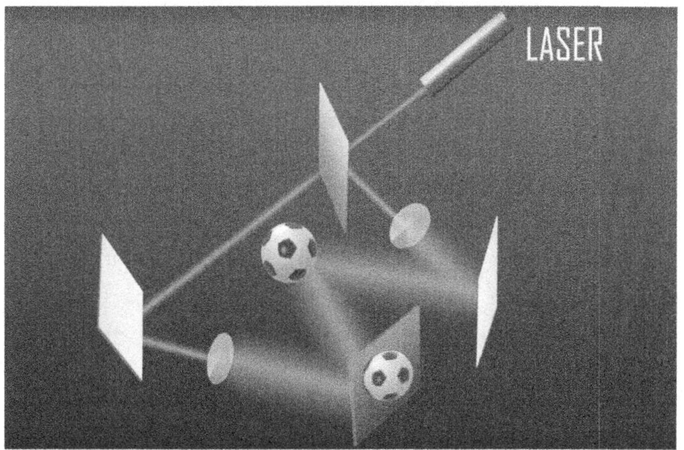

This diagram illustrates how a hologram is formed. We're shining a laser through a semi-opaque mirror, which splits the beam into two paths. The laser then widens,

[47] Hariharan, P. (2002). Basics of Holography. Cambridge University Press.

essentially becoming its own light mirror. Remember, light is a frequency, and frequencies carry information.

These laser beams carry information of the images they bounce off, which can be read if captured at the same distance from where the original image was reflected. When you take the other split light and reflect that diffused laser off the same final plate, its reflection also bounces off the image and reflects the information onto the screen plate. This process creates a 3-dimensional image.

It's a complex concept, I know. If you're finding it challenging to visualize (as I did initially), I highly recommend watching the video explanation available in the Life Gamer (LG) Resources section of the LTUVG app, under "Holograms Explained." It breaks down this fascinating process in a way that's easier to grasp.

This understanding of how holograms work is crucial as we delve deeper into the concept of our reality, potentially being holographic in nature. The idea that you can create the whole from just one part of the interference pattern that makes up the hologram, can be seen in aspects of our lives.

A gaming example of this is in *No Man's Sky*, which was a revolutionary game that has eighteen quintillion planets, wild, using a special kind of math that creates entire planets and ecosystems from tiny bits of code. Even if you visit one part of a planet, the game can recreate the whole planet's look and feel from this small bit of information. This is similar to a small piece of a hologram which can recreate a "fuzzier" version of the whole image.

A real-life example of holographic principles in action is found in one of the most important parts of our body: the brain. If you haven't heard of this before, you're not alone. When I picked up the book "The Holographic Universe" by Michael Talbot, I was enthralled. Talbot discusses the groundbreaking work of physicist David Bohm and neurophysiologist Karl Pribram, who independently developed holographic models of the universe and the brain, respectively.[48]

Pribram's holographic brain theory emerged from his studies on memory and brain function. He observed that even when significant portions of the brain were damaged or removed in humans, rats, or monkeys—including parts of the hippocampus—memories often remained intact. When Pribram learned about holograms, he saw an immediate connection to his work. He proposed that memories, like the information in a hologram, are not localized but distributed throughout the brain.

As Talbot explains, "If a hologram of a rose is cut in half and then illuminated by a laser, each half will still be found to contain the entire image of the rose. Indeed, even if the halves are divided again, each snippet of film will always be found to contain a smaller but intact version of the original image." Pribram suggested that the brain operates on similar principles, storing

---

[48] Talbot, M. (1991). The Holographic Universe. HarperCollins Publishers.

information in a distributed, hologram-like manner. How wild is that!

I know you probably think that this was all the evidence I had up my sleeve. Actually, the final judge on whether this is a holographic universe is you. For if this is a holographic universe, and we are just projections of consciousness in an illusory (and very real feeling) world, where does that consciousness come from? How does it communicate with us? Where does the voice inside your head come from? The voice that you hear when you are reading this book. Is that you, or is that coming from inside of you? What is the voice of your conscience, the voice that tells you to forgive, to let go of control, or that everything will work out if we just let it?

For myself, this voice comes from the controller of my Universe. My higher self. It's the voice that's guided me to many successful outcomes in life. It's what channeled this book. A major part of the game of life, what we are practicing in this book, is how to clear the interference between your controller and you, with the thousands of thoughts you have a day. The methods I'm teaching you are the same methods I used to clear and quiet my analytical mind, so that you too can receive guidance from your higher self.

At this moment, I'm currently maxing out my XP daily. I'm still working "full time" in finance, with my business partner using these principles to live in his purpose and expand the business so that we can pursue my dream in helping the world heal itself. My wife just received funding for a new mobile salt cave concept in Atlanta, we are co-running an international retreat space in Ecuador that is growing, and I finished this book in under nine months with the help of divine people like Josh Sprague. We are also living abundantly and sharing it with our community so they can have a safe haven.

My wife Zai'Ra asked me tonight, "What is your secret desire (in the work we do)?" I sheepishly said, "For world peace, it's secret because it's so cliche that it has to be covert." She laughed, and said hers was, "to be a role model for others to be their best selves in the world." This is why I love her, because we complete each other's statements. To achieve world peace, or paradise on earth as I like to call it, we must emulate it within ourselves first.

This is why service to others is so important. It grounds you so even while you are wildly successful, you realize that it is to help others also become wildly successful. At a minimum, by living example, holding that vibration sends that information out into the Universe, like a hologram.

MISSION 9: THE PERMISSION ROSE: Y OUR MULTIDIMENSIONAL BOUNDARY

Let's try our first exercise at creating something with our imagination. This is where things start to blossom and get really fun. Thus far, you've moved through some difficult soul work, but it's been for a purpose. To set the foundation for the fun parts. This is NOT easy, and you are AMAZING for making it this far into this Imagination Realization game.

Go to the LTUVG App, and enjoy this opportunity to level up your imagination, with the Permission Rose, your multidimensional boundary.

Mission 9 Activated

Open the LTUVG App and access Mission 9:
The Permission Rose: Your Multidimensional Boundary

As we close out another amazing chapter in your growth and expansion, this analogy really stuck with my wife when thinking about the permission rose. The permission rose is not a hard boundary, it's a flexible and fluid boundary. It's flexible because it is adaptable. Imagine that the rose is setting permissions like on a Google Doc. When you share a Google Doc, you have full control over who can view, comment, or edit the document. Some don't have access at all.

We can set our permission to interact with others' energy fields, always maintaining a healthy distance. Sometimes we set our permission roses to only allow those who mean our highest good to interact with us. We don't have to spend energy keeping them out of our space. Our rose will maintain our energy field and alert us if something needs adjustment or more attention. The permission rose is always between you and the other person, even when you are allowing them to give you a hug, you are giving them permission to share fields at that moment.

It's also flexible so that other people's auras don't bump up against something hard and rigid. When one encounters a rigid boundary, consciously or unconsciously, they also become rigid. Which is why typically people who set a lot of boundaries can come off as being rigid, still attracting confrontations that they'd probably rather avoid. With our permission rose, we can set permissions so that someone who doesn't respect boundaries will just naturally flow away from our energy field. Keeping your boundaries flexible allows you to flow through life easier, avoiding unnecessary encounters while still connecting with others in a genuine and authentic way.

Just like setting permissions on a Google Doc ensures your document remains safe and your work is respected, setting your permission rose helps maintain your energetic field. It ensures that your personal space is honored, and interactions with others are managed in a way that allows you to stay centered and level up efficiently. By visualizing and setting your permission rose, you're taking an active step in managing your energy, empowering you to easily interact with the subtle energy realm and be the observer of your world.

SAVE POINT 2 - REVIEW AND ASSESS

We've come to the end of the first arch of this journey. By now you have accumulated a ton of XP, journaled the Gems of Understanding that you've received, and you love yourself more! Life should feel a bit more challenging because you are leveling it up, but it should also be simpler. If you've lost friends or a job in the process, the Universe is just clearing out things so that it can bring you the resources to support your highest path. Let's do a quick review of the tools you have and in what scenario they are helpful.

Go check your LTUVG app and go to the Save Point 2 mission. There you will find access to your first Skill Codex I, providing a "quick reference" of each skill, the benefits, what it levels up, the gaming analogy, and when to use it. While you are at this save point, if you want to do another V.I.S.A. Skill Assessment, it might be a suitable time to check in on how much you've leveled up!

! Save Point 2: !

Review & Assess Unlocked
Go to LTUVG App

Be sure to check in with the app for a quick reference so you can familiarize yourself with each tool and how they benefit your individual skill trees. The more you focus on activities that earn XP for your weak points, the faster you will grow overall. Similar to Destiny, ESO or Diablo, think of it as balancing out your armor pieces so that your character has no weak spots.

You are only as strong as your weakest link.

The question marks in the "skill tree" section refers to skill trees that you haven't unlocked yet! As you progress through the manual, you will unlock additional Codex's that will reveal the skill trees that these activities also benefit. So, keep going and you'll discover what they are.

If you are up to the challenge (in vulnerability), here is a "secret" optional quest. It's not so secret because I'm telling you about it, but if you are still getting comfortable with the discomfort of the topics above, I suggest practicing an activity you've already unlocked instead. If not, let's go down this "secret" tunnel to see what's on the other side.

As always, the game of life is for YOU to play. What makes the journey so beautiful is when we remember to have fun.

Or, if you'd rather hear an incredible tale of how my beloved Zai'Ra and I journeyed to Mordor and survived to tell the tale, skip ahead to Level 2.

SECRET QUEST 10 - CONNECTING WITH THE DESTINY ORACLE

Take a deep breath in, release, push out the air, inhale again, deeper still, and release fully. Imagine this:

You wake up on a sunny Saturday morning, excited about your day, ready to engage in one of the new skills you've gained, starting with maybe some breathwork and then a short meditation, but what to meditate on? Wouldn't it be nice to have a quick reference of missions relevant to what would help you most in life for that day? This mission provides that tool but requires connecting with your intuition and being vulnerable enough to listen.

This upcoming activity is our first attempt at going a little deeper, and I trust if you are reading this, then you trust discomfort as a sign you are on the right path. Spread your wings of vulnerability to use the winds of discomfort to soar above your problems in life. Just like wings, being vulnerable is all about putting yourself out there authentically and risk missing the mark. Vulnerability is what allows you to get infinitely better, because as long as you try again, if you gave it your best, or worst, at least you tried.

This feeling blossomed within me years ago. It's a wild story.

I was finishing my course in the Silva Ultramind Method and learning how to remote-view into random people who had injuries. Remote viewing is the ability to gather information through the subtle energy realm utilizing extrasensory perception (ESP), similar to accessing a computer remotely but with your intuition instead.

I had made an agreement with a friend who is a trainer (Carla), who got her clients' permission to send me their first name, age, gender, and general location. For example, "Barbara, fifty-six, Brooklyn, female". I would close my eyes, activate my "centering exercise," an upgraded version of the grounding exercise (something you will learn later), and visualize that person's aura. I would see colors, energy flowing, and follow the energy to a part of their body. Based on the color or the area, I would intuitively share my assessment with Carla. To be clear, this information was not going back to the client, this was just an exercise to see if my remote viewing was accurate. Carla would only say two things in response, "Good job, that's accurate!" or "I don't have information on that." It could also be a combination of the two depending on the response.

If I'm being completely honest, it took some time for me to ask my friend if she would do this. That's because, at the time, being "wrong" was very uncomfortable for me. Over time, I've learned that the goal in life is to let go of being "right" or "wrong," for the truth needs no defense, but I digress. The point is, many of us would agree with the statement, "Being wrong in public can be very embarrassing." This experience pushed me into that area of discomfort. And this is how I grew from it.

I eventually surrendered to the assignment and decided to have fun with it. If Carla laughed at my intuitive "guesses" at least we'd have something funny to talk about. Her first client was Greg, forty-five, male from Queens. I centered myself, closed my eyes, and saw red energy in the back of an overweight male, moving lethargically. Verbatim, I wrote the following:

"Herniated disk in back? Weight gain/out of shape due to lack of ability to work around injury?"

And I hit send... I waited two excruciating hours for her response. Only to see...

"Yesss!!!! That's so accurate I want to hear what you saw in your vision! It's so amazing!!"

I had to sit down and take a moment. I still get chills from the excitement, because I then got another three clients.

Krystal, her next client, had pain in the knees and hips, and a sense of joint pain/arthritis. A very capable person, yet self-doubt is limiting her progress. No joke, two clients in a row, accurate with a high degree of confidence. I was ecstatic.

The next two clients, I was accurate on both as well, although I had to rescan the last client twice to get an accurate read. I've posted text evidence of this experience in the app for funsies. At this point, if you are reading the book, I imagine you can use your intuition to get a sense of whether this is possible or not, but just in case you are still skeptical, I want to be fully transparent so there is no shadow of a doubt of the legitimacy of this practice.

The amazing thing is that as you continue to build up XP in these areas of your V.I.S.A., you too can unlock this potential within you.

This next secret mission is designed to further activate your own intuitive gifts. Let's jump into this next activity that will give you a tool that you can use to practice communicating with intuitiveness.

SECRET MISSION 10: UNLOCKING YOUR GALACTIC COMPASS

For today's special mission, we tap into our intuition combined with the help of some ancient technology and use some current technology as a bridge.

iPhone users will need to download *13:20:sync*, and Android users will need to download Dreamspell. After you've downloaded either app, go to the LTUVG app and load today's mission.

Fair warning, 13:20:sync does cost $4, but it will be the best four dollars you've spent all year.

Mission 10 Activated
Open the LTUVG App and access Mission 10:
Unlocking Your Galactic Compass

Remember I talked about doing daily missions in Destiny or any game that gives bonuses for logging in daily and doing missions (*Elder Scrolls*, *Clash of Clans*, etc.)? Think of your morning Imagination Realization gaming sessions as an opportunity to practice the "daily energy" you need to embody to level up the most for that day. Whether it's vulnerability, intuition, service to others, or presence, your new Universal Compass will advise you. This can easily double your XP earned per activity by preparing you for the day's challenges that will come up!

Let's say the day is a *Blue Spectral Night* day, whose combined energy is:

I Dissolve in order to Dream
Releasing Intuition
I seal the Input of Abundance
With the Spectral tone of Liberation
I am guided by my own power (Abundance) doubled

Without going too much into detail, from reading this, you might pick up that surrendering control (dissolve/release) and listening to your intuition and following your dreams could create abundance in your day.

If I knew that, then maybe I should practice my intuition detection skills after some breathwork. I would also focus on going with the flow in my day and not try to control or force things to happen in my day; trusting that abundance will flow easily and effortlessly. I can name several occasions where being prepared for the day in this way has brought in more abundance for Zai'Ra and I.

It's like going to a concert and preparing by listening to the songs of the artist before you go, so you can sing the words when you hear it live. It's worth it because you'll only get one chance to sing the songs live with the artist, and then the moment passes you by.

Similarly, aligning with the Tzolkin calendar each day may not always sync you with the events that will happen during the day, but they will certainly give you a better chance at maxing out your XP each day than if you didn't. If you made it through this level, try to connect with the calendar each day to guide your daily missions from the book, and feel free to connect with the mantra I created that is channeled from the Galactic Signature of that day in our community emails.

Don't forget the Life Game Resources section of the app for more information on the Tzolkin Calendar.

IMPORTANT! Once you submit the special journal entry for this mission, you'll unlock a special Guild! The "Galactic Navigator's Guild" Channel is a private forum where I will provide additional guidance 3 days a week on the galactic signature of the day. It's also a place where you can ask questions and share your own experiences. Enjoy!

Level 3 Recap:

- Subtle Energy Skills Unlocked:
    - Permission Rose: Your Multidimensional Compass
- Universal Tools Acquired:
    - Earthing for Earthlings
    - Grounding Grounds Me Meditation
    - The Galactic Compass

LEVEL 4

OUR HEALING STORY

TRUE LOVE AT FIRST SIGHT

Before we take a deep dive into the rest of the skills, I want to tell you how this book even came about. This also creates space to build your daily practices and new skills to settle into your body.

Why am I sharing these radical ideas with you now and with such conviction? It's because I'm living a magical life full of miracles! And not alone. My life partner, wife, and best friend, Zai'Ra, was the first place where this magic began to happen! We were both studying shamanism and energy work before the destined day we met, but the true fireworks didn't erupt until we met, six bliss-filled years ago.

I hope you are ready for a love story that transpired into an even bigger miracle than my father's. First, we must go back to our fateful reunion.

"Enjoy adventures? Let's go!"

This was the tagline on Zai'Ra's profile that initially sparked my interest. I LOVED adventures and was looking for a life partner to go on epic adventures with. The dating app we met on was called The League and, as the story goes, she swiped right on me one time and then put the app away. Seriously. In many circles, she's referred to me as the "one-swipe wonder." When I swiped on her, and we began texting, it truly was a fairy tale story. Not without its moments of vulnerability and risks, which is what made our trust fall into unconditional love that much more intense.

I remember it like it was yesterday. My opening text to her was casual. I hit her with a, "What inspires you?" Her response was nearly a paragraph long, where she shared her short-term motivation as well as her long-term vision for the future. I was enthralled with her answers, hanging onto every word of her response, only wanting more. I'm a romantic, what can I say? Her vision for her future was also aligned with my own, and I wrote back an equally long paragraph.

For the record, her girlfriend advised her not to send me long text messages, but I loved them, and she loved mine. Not necessarily what a dating expert would advise, but I never listened to them anyway. By the fourth or fifth text exchange, we touched on shamanism. It was here that I intentionally redirected our conversation. I was, SO EXCITED. "She's perfect!" I thought, and I redirected the convo because I just wanted to see her in person and go deep, with our conversation.

When we met in person, it was what I had waited lifetimes for. Short window, we had set up the day perfectly. It was a Thursday, she didn't work on Friday, and I could get out of work early. I was nervous, she was nervous, we'd been texting for two weeks leading up to this, so there was plenty of pressure. I remember seeing her walk into the restaurant, the sun hitting her face, hearing beautiful theme music in the background (in my head). When she sat down, we immediately connected. The conversation went from her incredible accolades in life, prowess as a track star, to her deep care for her family and friends. If you ever meet her, you will feel how special a star she is, inside and out.

On our inaugural eight-hour first date, the moment I knew just how special she was when I had asked about her parents, assuming she was raised in a stable home because of her amazing qualities. As tragedy would have it, due to unexpected deaths on both her mom's and dad's side, her parents weren't able to be there for her. She effectively raised her sister during their teen years and started her first business when she was twelve mowing lawns to help support her family.

A shining moment for our journey is that she and her parents have healed from those tough moments and are closer than ever. Another testament to our sacred union. Let this be an inspiration for you and your family, that by healing yourself, you can create the opportunity for transformational ancestral healing as well. But back to our first date.

It was when we started talking about the trauma she experienced during her upbringing that I reached over to hold her hand, letting her know that she was safe. When our hands touched, it was electric, galactic. I felt our entire lives flash in front of my eyes, and I fell in love. Each date after that was at least six hours. We couldn't get enough of each other's energy.

We eventually did talk about shamanism and the gift that it had shown us on each of our journeys. In fact, for her next birthday, I gifted her a seven-week soul retrieval course with the renowned shaman and author I mentioned earlier, Itzhak Beery. If you remember, this was the same course that I had taken with Itzhak four years prior, what a coincidence! At the end of this two-month course, Zai'Ra was, like me, chosen "randomly" by Itzhak for a one-on-one soul retrieval. What we witnessed was ancestral healing of the parental wounds that had plagued her childhood.

You see, Zai'Ra had recently been diagnosed with a blood autoimmune disease called Lupus, which has no clinical "cure". She was diagnosed after a life of trauma and separation from her family, as well as some recent painful experiences in her personal life. Through the pain, diagnosis, and difficult news that she may not ever be as active as she once was, Zai'Ra was upbeat and confident she would find a way through it. She did.

Her loving, caring, intelligent, brave, curious, and compassionate nature remained true. Despite the people in her life who tried to take advantage of that kindness. She is a pure soul that nothing in this life could tarnish. In seeing this, I was convinced that it was this suffering from other people creating this disease in her body. That she could be cured if she cleansed these energies from her. Together, we were determined to find a cure for her dis-ease. This soul retrieval ceremony was a major step in that process.

The next magical experience was a painful one, but one that even to this day, gives me goosebumps recalling.

For those unfamiliar with lupus, it's a chronic autoimmune disease that can affect various parts of the body, including the skin, joints, kidneys, brain, and other organs. Some lupus patients, particularly those with antiphospholipid antibodies, may require blood thinners to prevent blood clots. Blood clots are dangerous because they can break up and flow directly into the heart causing a stroke, heart attack, or worse.

The double-edged sword of blood thinners is that your blood doesn't naturally coagulate, which puts you at risk of uncontrollable bleeding from an injury (even a small one). Because of this risk, doctors advise being less active, which again, was a big part of Zai'Ra's life. It also makes things like surgery or having kids way more complicated. We were concerned about bleeding to death or risking clots if you go off the meds for these procedures. That isn't a way to live!

Even with the blood thinners, lupus patients still get hit with these nasty things called "flare-ups." Zai'Ra described it to me like this:

"It feels like your skin is turning into cement and you are being inescapably electrocuted from the inside of your body."

Yea, to put it plainly, your own body becomes a torture chamber.

Fast forward a month from Zai'Ra's soul retrieval, and I come home to her being in excruciating pain. "Oh no," I think, "A flare-up!" It was the first time that I had seen her in this kind of pain, and I remember being infuriated when the hospital told her, "If the pain gets worse, come back tomorrow." We had no choice but to ride out the storm at home.

She fell asleep with tears in her eyes, me holding her in my arms with an obsidian crystal in my hand over her belly where a lot of the pain was. Tears welled up in my eyes as well. "This can't be happening," I thought.

The love of my life is suffering in all of this pain. I didn't know what to do, so I just said to myself, "I will do anything to take her pain away." This became my mantra that I kept repeating until I fell asleep like a lullaby.

"I'll do anything to take Zai'Ra's pain away..."

What happened next was like a CGI cutscene in a video game. As I dozed off and entered my dream state, I found myself in the middle of a storm, literally. Like Peter Pan, I was flying through a storm, and I could see a ship off in the distance being thrown by the sea. I didn't know why, but I knew that I needed to get to that ship. Fighting through the wind, rain and lightning, I soared through the air until I landed on the ship. As I caught my bearings, I immediately ran to the main cabin and threw open the door. Just like a rescue mission, I saw Zai'Ra curled on the bed, writhing in pain. Startled by the noise, she jolted up and looked at me.

When our eyes locked, it was as if I was looking at her in the physical realm. Shocked, I woke up. When I opened my eyes, she was looking at me as well!

She stammered, "Did you just see me?"

I replied shockingly, "Were you just in my dream?"

Even more surprised she screeched, "Wait, you saw me too?"

We were struck with amazement. We had done journeying in shamanism, but nothing like this. It would be the equivalent to thinking you were playing *Zelda* by yourself, and then all of a sudden it turned into an MMORPG, and you met your best friend in the game. Shocking and exciting AF!

Forgetting about the pain she was in, we both agreed to meet each other back in the subtle energy realm and dropped back into our journeys. Lo and behold, we successfully found each other again!

When I returned to the ship in the storm, I took the pain that was plaguing her and flew off into the storm to take it as far away from her as possible. I didn't really think through the process of getting rid of it, but I remember taking it into the storm. It was in that moment that I lost consciousness within the dream. From Zai's point of view, her journey ended with her waking up on a beach, walking on the sand, holding my hand. The storm had passed. Or so we thought.

When I finally opened my eyes in the morning, I felt a slow rumbling in my stomach, and then an immediate cramp. I ran into the bathroom, knowing that I had something in my stomach that had to come out. As I sat on my iron throne, I thought it must have been something I ate the previous night that didn't agree with me. After about fifteen minutes of no movement except for an exponential increase in pain, I realized that Zai'Ra would probably need to go to work before I made it out of the bathroom. I mustered up the pain tolerance to yell, "Babe, I will see you later, love you."

I wish I was exaggerating, but to this day I have never felt that much pain in my life, and I am not unfamiliar with pain. I played collegiate-level football, nearly died colliding with the pavement going 100 mph on a motorcycle and have been coined accident-prone for much of my life.

It was around minute twenty on the toilet that I asked the Universe, "What is going on?" I was in excruciating pain, but nothing was coming out! I said to myself, "I'll do anything to make this pain go away." In a flash, the prior night came right back to me.

"I thought you said you'd do anything to take her pain away?"

This sarcastic internal voice reminded me of what I had promised. My higher self has to be sassy sometimes so that I'll listen to obvious messages. This might happen to you as well. "You said you'd do anything to take her pain away, prove it," I heard again, this time less sarcastic, and more direct. I intuitively understood that this foreign pain in my intestines was a transfer of Zai'Ra's pain from the night before. "Idiot!" I thought to myself. "Of course! When I took the pain from her and didn't release it into the ocean, it attached to me."

After that realization, I knew what to do. I had to finish the job and release it from you know where. With determination to see Zai'Ra healed, I made a makeshift squatty potty with the trashcan and plunger and released the darkness into the depths of the sewers of Harlem. After the dust had settled, like most people, I wanted to see how big it was. It was so painful; I was convinced it was the size of a submarine.

Boy the Universe has such a good sense of humor sometimes, because as I slowly peered beyond the edges of the toilet, I saw this four-inch-long, quarter-inch-wide sliver of pure darkness. It literally was the color of charcoal—dark, sooty charcoal. Seriously. Excited, not at all embarrassed, I ran out of the bathroom to explain the situation to Zai'Ra.

I showed her the toothpick of darkness. She was shocked, and also grateful. Because the pain that she had the night before had never passed this quickly. It also never came back again, for as long as we have been together. The crazy part of this entire story is that we later would find out that clinically, the disease was no longer in her blood. That through soul retrieval and cleansing her life of the pain of her childhood, her body healed itself from lupus! But I'll save that miraculous story for much later.

Since that moment, we were hooked on shamanism and other healing modalities to heal ourselves and share it with our loved ones. We dove headfirst into our love and our healing, trusting that despite all of the risks of making ourselves totally vulnerable, this was the best path to heal and thrive together.

We both had hidden our inner child deep in a castle inside our subconscious, due to the untimely deaths of our siblings, aunts, uncles, and a fractured family unit. If we were to rescue our inner children, we would have to let go of what we thought we knew about reality and trust in our love.

We truly believed that by healing ourselves, we would create the chance for our families to do the same thing. To date, this theory has continued to ring true, as you saw from our parents' experience. But how the heck did we end up in Ecuador in the first place? This is the next epic saga that I will cover.

TO MORDOR & BACK AGAIN

If you are a gamer, you are probably familiar with *Lord of The Rings*, and the journey of Frodo Baggins and Samwise Gamgee to Mordor to destroy the ring of power. If you have not read the books or seen the movie, it's way too long of a story for me to attempt to summarize, so I won't. I suggest googling or watching a summary of *Lord of the Rings*, or just listen to this story and it will give you an idea of the beautiful, painful, and heart-wrenching journey these two hobbits (halflings) took to save middle earth from evil by destroying a ring forged in hate. A ring that tempted anyone who touched it to turn to betray their good nature in exchange for power and literal invincibility. I love this tale, and I learned why I read it and watched it numerous times, so that I could survive my own journey to the barren lands of Mordor and back again.

This journey starts during the pandemic, COVID-19 in New York City. Certainly, a version of Mordor at that time. It was early 2020, Zai'Ra and I had just moved in with one another. Working in finance, I was considered "essential," so I had to ride my e-bike through a desolate Manhattan to work while most others stayed inside. The timing of the pandemic allowed Zai'Ra to work remotely, and shortly after, I took six months off to transition to a new company. We used this extra time to build a fun online community where I DJ'd, and Zai taught yoga on Twitch.

I send my prayers to every family who lost someone dear to them during COVID. At the same time, I am grateful for COVID. I am a firm believer that the millions of lives sacrificed during COVID allowed the survivors to do some deep reflections on their own purpose; while they were stuck inside, forced to pause their lives. It was also a glaring indicator that many people in America and around the world were suffering from mental health imbalances. This got Zai and me thinking: what do we want to do with our holistic healing practices? How best can we share our gifts with the world to support this mental health crisis?

We continued our studies and practices, co-creating online communities and experimenting with the Zoom world of exchanges online. As many remember, people were probably the most turtle-like they've ever been and also open to a new world of possibilities and experiences.

I was focused on love and had a burning desire. To marry Zai'Ra, the love of my life. Luckily, right before the world shut down, I made a trip up to Buffalo to buy a ring. Talk about serendipity. If you have proposed to someone, then you know that that ring was burning a hole in my closet, especially as our two-year anniversary approached. It was the perfect time to do it, but how? What was the best way to honor the love we had? As the stress of getting married began to rise within me, I began to break down mentally and emotionally. I picked fights with her for no apparent reason. I remember when I told Zai after one of those breakdowns, "I feel like we are falling apart." She responded with fire,

"No, YOU are falling apart, what is going on?"

Honestly, I didn't. I didn't know what was going on. I was unaware of my insecurities that were being activated, causing me to get upset, angry, and snap at Zai'Ra. It was unlike me. Which made it even that much more worrisome.

I used my shamanism practices and journeyed into it. The answer came back loud and clear, I was afraid. Afraid that my future marriage with Zai'Ra would end in divorce like my parents' relationship. To prevent this from happening, I was sabotaging the relationship before it even reached that point.

Have you ever self-sabotaged in your life? Or seen anyone you know sabotage their own lives? Maybe taking a traumatic event and unconsciously replicating it out of fear of it happening again?

When we have unhealed trauma that still lives in our body, it finds a way to the surface. Activating those levels so we have the chance to clear them and heal. Evidence of this can be found in Dr. Jonathan Shay's work with combat veterans. In his book *Achilles in Vietnam*, he describes a veteran named Fred who became extremely agitated and engaged in self-destructive activities around the anniversary of his own traumatic combat experience. One particularly harrowing incident involved Fred driving his motorcycle at over 100 mph on winding mountain roads, as if he was invincible, narrowly avoiding death.

This pattern continued until the underlying trauma was addressed through therapy. After processing his trauma, Fred was able to break this cycle of anniversary reactions and risky behaviors.[49]

How did I break through my own cycle? Plant medicine.

---

[49] Shay, J. (1994). Achilles in Vietnam: Combat Trauma and the Undoing of Character. Scribner.

Itzhak used to joke often, "Don't trust a new shaman sharing plant medicine out of their basement in Brooklyn." I wish I had remembered that before we ended up meeting a woman we will refer to as "Shar."

She was actually in our apprenticeship course with Itzhak. When we met in late 2020, there was something mystical about her. One day, after a recent blow up with Zai, I asked Itzhak about plant medicine and its benefits. He himself was a shaman who did not administer plant medicine, but he did partner with some who did. They unfortunately were all in South America, and during COVID they were inaccessible.

Shar must have seen the disappointment on my face, because after the class was over, she side-chatted me, "I am administering ancient plant medicine ceremonies if you are interested." This did intrigue me, was it Ayahuasca? Or was it some other plant medicine I hadn't heard of? It was less than a month until our anniversary, and I was still unsettled and afraid.

So, I scheduled a Zoom call with Shar to get a read on what she was offering. She said all the right things that were aligned with Zai'Ra and my principles. That the medicine came from an authentic shaman, that she practiced for multiple years and trained in Costa Rica and in Bedford, NY before offering her first ceremony. With little hesitation, I signed both Zai and myself up, and we were set for a life-altering experience. The next ceremony was only ten days before our anniversary, time was ticking!

In *Lord of the Rings*, this was the moment when Frodo and Samwise promised Gandalf they would meet Strider at the inn with the ring of power. It was supposed to be just a simple hand off. But one night at the Prancing Pony, their peaceful lives changed forever when the Ringwraiths attacked them. The hobbits suddenly found themselves in an epic quest, just as Zai'Ra and I were about to embark on our own surprise adventure.

Finally, it was the night of the ceremony. As Zai and I sat down in Shar's loft on the lower east side, the air felt different. A sunny day soon turned stormy as Shar was setting the intention for the circle. Thunder and lightning began to rumble until it crescendoed into a deafening crack that shook the room; just as Shar finished blessing the four directions and the medicine.

"Whoa, this is gonna be special," Zai'Ra and I simultaneously thought while looking at each other. We had no idea what kind of ride this new medicine was going to take us on. We were equally excited and scared at the same time.

As the thunder continued to echo around us, we were beckoned to approach Shar and consume the tea of Kanna, the ancient medicine we were offered. Roots of a succulent in South Africa, this medicine was designed to bring you into pure bliss, such that you can let go of the traumas you think make you who you are. As one lets go of their stories, it allows them to see who they were always meant to be. Melting the shroud of traumas around them so that they can stand in their full power and be as bright as the star that they came from.

This is the goal, after years of ceremonies, to attain. For Zai'Ra though? Well, this is exactly what her first experience was like. It was miraculous. Like Captain Marvel shining with the energy of a supernova, Zai'Ra erupted into a beam of light in the middle of the ceremony floor. She was dancing to the incredible soundtrack guiding our journey, smiling and flowing. It was an incredible distraction for me. Because otherwise, my journey was a nightmare.

Death by tragedy, including suicide, has plagued my dad's side of the family. Aside from the loss of my younger sister and brother, my closest aunt and uncle both passed away tragically at a young age. I had contemplated suicide at a young age during my parents' divorce, and a sibling had shared with me that they, too, had ideated suicide recently. It was devastating.

These fears manifested themselves in my journey with Kanna as I saw all of us being swept into a tornado of death by ego. Then in the eye of the storm, I saw my grandfather. I associated him with a lot of the pain that I felt because of toxic masculinity which had plagued him and my family, as it does most of society. When my grandfather suddenly passed away, my dad and his siblings broke down, self-destructing. Picking fights and hurting one another emotionally and physically. My grandmother passed the following year, resulting in more heart break. She was the core of our family unit, known as "Big Mama." After her loss, many family members forgot how to have compassion with one another and things still haven't healed completely over a decade later.

I kept asking my grandfather, on the journey, to let go of his pain, to be more open-hearted. I blamed him for the chaos that was ensuing in our family.

To be clear, my grandfather was a great man, but not without his own flaws. A black man who grew up in Texas with the Jim Crow laws, he moved his family to South Central LA for a "safer" life. While they struggled to overcome their situation, my grandfather would have four children with four different women outside of the core of their family unit. Despite the pain of betrayal this caused, my grandmother, with a heart of mass proportions, helped raise many of those children.

"Even if they aren't from me, we are family."

She was a superwoman, and I thank her often for teaching her kids the gift of unconditional love.

I attempted to communicate with my grandfather the pain he had left behind, the multiple strokes my grandma had before her passing, the early deaths of his children, and the pain that still lived within all of us, even me. I admonished him for not having the strength to face the damage that he'd caused in his life. I was frustrated with him. It was a very intense experience, something like a "boss level" that I will share in more detail later on.

The next morning, when we were in our closing circle, sharing our experiences and how we felt, I saw Zai'Ra, and she was full of light. It was so beautiful to see. Then

I looked at myself, and I felt pathetic. Not worthy of her love, and I blamed my grandfather for that as well.

When we went home, I carried this feeling with me, and the storm picked back up from the previous evening. So much that it broke open our windows and woke me up as the window knocked over my expensive speaker near my DJ setup. Still in this emotional funk, I had to clean up the mess and make sure no water got into the gear. I was also planning on using my DJ controller as a part of my proposal, and during COVID, if any equipment got broken, replacing it would take weeks or months. Time check, we are six days until my proposal so this stuff CANNOT get ruined. Perfect setup for me to get triggered and pick a fight.

Zai'Ra was helpful while we cleaned up the mess, still in her cheery mood. As she cleaned, I could feel frustration building up in me. I was having trouble communicating how she could help without blowing up on her for doing something wrong while helping. I then got mad at myself. "It isn't her fault this happened, she's just helping, why am I being short with her?" I asked myself.

Then I had a flashback. I remembered that this was how my dad felt when he made a mistake, and we were trying to help. There was one time he forgot an envelope with a lot of money somewhere, rent money and then some. The wrong thing to do at that moment was to try to make him feel better. As a result, we were walking on eggshells for the entire day for fear that we might do something wrong and be on the receiving end of his frustration. If you've gone through this in your life too, it's okay, you aren't alone.

As I came back to the moment with Zai, I realized that it wasn't my grandfather who didn't have the strength to face his fears, it was me! I needed to have the courage to face my own fears and to choose to love instead! I remembered the mantra that I've told you:

Life isn't happening to me; it's happening for me. To learn from, to grow from.

With this realization, I also accepted that I needed another ceremony if I were going to have a chance at being the authentic person Zai'Ra deserved to have as her husband. I booked a private session with Shar for the following evening, with the acknowledgement that my grandfather's mistakes would only weigh on me if I didn't choose to forgive him, accept him, as well as myself. From there, I didn't know where the journey would take me, but I knew that was the starting point...or was it?

I rode down to Shar's with Zai'Ra's hand in mine, like our first date. She was dropping me off for the biggest mission of my life. To rid myself of ancestral trauma and step into my true essence so I could spend the rest of my life with the woman of my dreams. As Zai'Ra gave me a hug and kiss, and I rang the buzzer for the apartment, I could feel the tension building within me. "This time tomorrow, I will be healed!" I told myself, "Cured of this dis-ease that is standing in the way of being my blissful self."

And then doubt started to seep in, "Could you actually be strong enough to..." To what? I wasn't actually sure. Was it to let go? But let go of what? Ego? Pride? Control? All of them?

"What if I let go of everything and nothing changes?"

I feared. Then what? "Don't let those thoughts seep in," I told myself, almost chastising.

"You are going to see yourself as Zai'Ra sees herself, as she sees you."

For context, how she "saw" herself after her first ceremony is something incredibly rare. It takes the courage to see all the dark places in your soul and accept them, so you can shine with the 100 percent luminance of your wholeness. She had accessed that truth with one sip. I had to get there.

I knew where I needed to go, what I was calling in; the only difficulty was that in order to get to the promised land, I had to set my destination and then let go of the need to get there. That all of this effort might just be a step in my evolutionary path, but an arrival might not be reached, and that's okay. "Easier said than done," I thought, fighting off my need to control. I grounded myself, saw a positive outcome, and then let go of the details. "Here we go."

As the sun set over the Manhattan skyline, Shar set down a container and four pieces of paper in front of me. "What are these for?" I asked myself. As if reading my thoughts, she explained that from my first ceremony, we had determined that there were four pillars propping up the false idea of who I was: the false sense of self standing in the way of my true self. She advised that I write the four things down before drinking the medicine and then choose which to burn first. I took a moment to write down what I remembered, trying to simply "surrender and trust."

The first words were unbalanced ego, the voice inside my head that wants more attention and validation. The projection of my false self.

The second word was control, the desire to control all of the things around me to keep people safe and guide the ship where I thought it was supposed to go. The need for things to go "my way."

The third words were guilt/shame, for the pain that I had caused in the past to almost every woman that I said I loved. This is the guilt that caused me to self-destruct and repeat the experiences I wanted to break away from.

The fourth word was awareness, or lack thereof. Oftentimes I would act with intention, without considering impact. I assumed that my way of thinking was the most appropriate. My lack of awareness also could do the opposite, allowing others to take advantage of me or those I cared about.

These were deep pillars that I had to somehow knock out all in one night. But which to start with?

As I considered each one carefully, Shar instructed me to approach the altar, while she blessed the medicine. I then gave my gratitude, said an internal intention, and drank the medicine. I returned to my seat and began to meditate on each word. Within the first moment of closing my eyes, I heard the word "control," and immediately went to grab the word and throw it in the fire. But then I froze. I remembered that I had told myself I had to "let" the journey come to me. The answer should come to me, I had to be patient so that my true self could tell me. Chasing it, a pattern in my life, would only make it run away faster. I sat and waited for the message...

I think this was supposed to be a ten-to-fifteen-minute exercise, and as I sat there, I recalled Shar walking around me slowly, sharing different messages to help to inspire me. I remained sitting listening for a clear message from the subtle energy realm. The funny thing about being in medicine is that time becomes a vortex where an hour can feel like fifteen minutes. I would later discover that it was about an hour later when she finally woke me up out of my thought loop. All I heard her say was,

"You must let go of control, so you can take full control of yourself."

Boom. An explosion of consciousness erupted inside of my mind, heart, and soul. It was as if I understood the source of all of my pain and trauma. I realized that I cared so much about my family, my loved ones, this planet, that I felt I truly needed to control everything to keep them safe. This is obviously impossible, but it fed an unbalanced ego that convinced me that I could protect everyone. It was in that instant that I remembered I wasn't doing it on my own. That I was leaving a huge part of the equation out of the solution, the Universe.

As I continued to unravel my control, questioning where it came from, I started to feel a sense of freedom approaching. I saw that the connection between all of the pillars holding up the facade of Christapher Benson, was control.

My attempt to be perfect so others wouldn't be harmed set impossible expectations. This stemmed from my childhood fear of making a mistake. I also covered up my own feelings in this process. That resulted in me lying when I was unable to meet those impossible expectations. When the truth eventually was uncovered, which ALWAYS happened, pain whiplashed, and I would feel shame and disappointment. This shame fed my own fears of disappointment, so I would then repeat the behavior of control to protect people from me! But if I pull control out of the equation, if I just am who I am, and trust that the Universe is guiding me on my path...

"Then it is control that is the source of my misery! ...in the FIRE you must go!"

I exclaimed. As soon as control was burning in the fire, I threw "unbalanced ego", shame/guilt, and lack of awareness into the fire too. It was incredibly freeing, like a rush of fresh air into my heart, mind, and soul.

The journey that ensued was like Aladdin's carpet ride through the happiest moments of my life. I felt that bliss that Sadhguru speaks of. It was like being in a hurricane until suddenly, with one epiphany, the storm ceased immediately. The rain quiets, clouds dissipate, the sun peers through the clouds, and you realize you were the one creating the storm. In one moment, I fully understood that the Universe was guiding me in the right direction all this time, it was me who was fighting the path. It wasn't that life was hard, it was that I was going against the grain.

As I relaxed into this ecstasy, Zai'Ra naturally popped into my mind. Marrying this amazing woman, how lucky am I? Then I realized that my "plan" to propose to her was not about her at all, it was about me! The plan was an online, very public surprise LIVE proposal on Twitch. There were a few things I hadn't considered, but the main one was that Zai is a very private person. She would much prefer a private setting to a public one, let alone broadcast it.

Normally, I would be in a place of denial and resistance rationalizing, "I'd already told everyone the plan! What will they say?" But in this bliss state everything is easy and crystal clear. I realized that what I should do was to plan a date with Zai'Ra in our favorite part of Central Park, under the trees, and have my best friend come take pictures and video so we could capture the moment. Then we could surprise our family by showing them the ring together, live on twitch.

Spoiler alert She said yes! The Central Park proposal was movie-worthy, supported by two incredible lifelong friends and nature's miracle of sunshine and trees. Between tears and sobs, I got down on both knees and admitted that I'd been chasing her through lifetimes so I could spend my life with her. That I would be honored for her to be my life partner, for her to take me as her husband and guardian, and that we could live in bliss together for the rest of our existence. She pulled me up and, with tears in her eyes, said yes. We danced and frolicked the rest of the day, floating on clouds. It was perfect.

I know you probably forgot that this love story was supposed to emulate *Lord of the Rings*, but we are getting there. I wish that I could tell you that after Zai'Ra and I were engaged, we continued to live out our days in Harlem, building a healing community doing humble work.

If that was how our journey ended, it would have no connection whatsoever to Mordor. There would have been no Sauron, no Saruman, or Shelob the spider.

However, after I had my epiphany about how to propose to Zai'Ra, Shar saw an opportunity to tempt my ego. She asked if I wanted another cup of medicine. "What could go wrong?" I thought. I took another cup, and innocent seeds of "saving the world" were planted within my subconscious so that I would throw all my savings, nearly $200k, into supporting Shar's work. Why? So that she could bring these magically transformative ceremonies to those who needed it, my friends and family included.

It became our "precious" illusion of paradise, and it almost cost us everything. I'll share the details of this harrowing tale in the upcoming chapters, but I'll leave you with this piece of advice.

"If a shaman, or healer, while guiding you in a vulnerable state, asks you for financial help of any kind, run..."

Shar indeed asked me if I would support her ceremonies while I was in her care. Instead of running away, I ran into the fire. And even though it was a journey to hell and back, I have no regrets.

I have no regrets because Zai'Ra and I survived and united through it all. Our purpose, love, inspiration, resolve, discernment, grace and forgiveness were laid bare from this grueling quest into darkness. It is because of this fool's errand that I can share these incredible abilities, skills and tools with you to activate in your own adventure (and in the safety of your own hobbit hole).

We used these skills to raise over $500k for The Warrior Sanctuary, build a beautiful healing community, work less and make more, while also transforming our lives to have the freedom we wanted. I share this cautionary tale to say,

"You have the ability to do all of the things we have done, and more."

As you utilize these practices consistently, your higher self will start to guide you to your highest vibrational path. The next chapter is where you begin to uncover the Universal Principles that govern your YOUniverse. There isn't a shadow of a doubt in the efficacy of these principles in unlocking massive amounts of experience points in your life.

The simple question is, as Morpheus said in *The Matrix*:

"Do you want to take the blue pill,
and return to your normal life,
Or do you want to take the red pill,
and see how deep the rabbit hole goes?"

The choice is yours, if you want to open the next chapter, and join us on this adventure of manifesting paradise on earth.

CLEANING HOUSE

As we step further into the world of subtle energy, it's important to remain curious about your inner world. With each new quest and ability, you uncover new experiences and unlock new abilities that only you will know. Please be an active member of the Life Gamer Guild community so that your victories and struggles can also support others on the journey. It will also help you level up for new missions and content and create the opportunity for me to support you in real time as those epiphanies happen. Who knows, sharing a story or struggle might lead to gaining a GOU! Just like a

MMORPG, it's the community that provides inspiration and support for us to keep leveling up our characters. It's a loving, growing, supportive family, and it's there for you.

Before we go any farther into the subtle energy realm, however, it is CRUCIAL that you establish cleansing practices to clear your energy. I've already suggested procuring sage or palo santo for your "gaming sanctuary," but as we level up these skills, we need to maintain cleanliness of our 5 bodies of consciousness that are utilizing these skills.

Just as you take a shower and brush your teeth daily, it's important to cleanse your energetic field daily as well. If you don't, the stagnant energy that sticks to you, just like used oil in a car, will affect your performance.

For example, if you are an empath, I'm sure you have noticed feeling drained or taking on someone else's energy. You may have also noticed that if an environment is demeaning, vampirical, or tends to find the "bad" in every moment, then you naturally don't "feel good" being there. My beloved was this way until she learned how to manage her energy. One of those is a tool we've already established, the permission rose, but because energy cannot be created or destroyed, only transformed, our permission roses also need cleansing, like a filter. And just like a filter, the more it filters, the sooner it needs to be replaced. These cleansing methods will help refresh your filters and cleanse your energy field so you can start each day fresh and anew, if you remember to do them.

A perfect example. I worked at a corporate desk in finance for over a decade before I met Zai'Ra. It was full of toxic masculinity, cursing, debauchery, yelling and berating. While the job nourished my bank account, the environment definitely did not nourish my soul.

One day, Zai asked me a question, and I barked an answer back at her like I would do at the trading desk. She paused, went to our meditation room, and brought some palo santo and asked if I'd cleanse my energy. I was so used to this that at first, I was defensive, saying, "I'm fine." As I opened my heart and dropped my guard, I realized she was right. One rule that helps me with cleansing:

You can never cleanse yourself too much.

If you feel resistance to cleansing yourself when you sit in your "gaming sanctuary," then you most likely NEED it. Negative energy that is sticking to us, just like a parasite, doesn't want to be released, so it will often create that resistance telling us "You don't need cleansing, you're good." Trust your intuition here, not your mind.

These practices have historical context and are thousands of years old, some dating back to the usage of salt by the Egyptians to cleanse themselves of energetic and physical dis-ease.[50]

---

[50] Cayce, E. (1997). *Edgar Cayce's Egypt: Psychic Revelations on the Most Fascinating Civilization Ever Known*. A.R.E. Press.

"The Egyptians were well aware of the multifaceted benefits of salt, utilizing it in their daily lives for purification, healing, and spiritual protection. Their advanced understanding of natural remedies was a testament to their deep connection with the earth and its resources."

Above all else, as we continue on this adventure, know that your energy is ALWAYS sovereign, it belongs to you, and nobody else can actually control or alter it. You can allow it to happen, consciously or unconsciously. This book is a reminder of how to call back all of your Gems of Understanding, so that you can collect these lost soul shards. These soul shards will then allow you to finally recover your inner child, who is still up in that castle waiting for you to rescue them.

We're going to think of these cleansing agents as levels of remedy potions. Depending on the level of each, it will clear certain status affects you have or what you want to call in.

<u>Common Remedy Potion</u> - Incense Sticks: Mood Setter. These are made from aromatic plant materials and essential oils, or candles. Great cleansing potion for beginners, offering a simple way to calm and call in the energy that the smell of incense attracts. Comes in different scents such as dragon's blood, Nag Champa, sandalwood, jasmine.

<u>Uncommon Remedy Potion</u> - Palo Santo: Cleanses and Resets Intention. Often called "holy wood," it is a sacred offering of trees in Central and South America. This is

your uncommon cleansing agent that will be your go-to in most situations. Can cleanse emotional energy that isn't too stuck and allow for positive intentions to be replaced. This is my go-to cleansing potion. It's portable and can also just help generally make situations better. We would use this in the office often to cleanse negative energy before it had time to stick to others.

Rare Remedy Potion - Sage: Purifies and Removes Negative Status Effect. An ancient herb known for its powerful purifying effects. If your uncommon remedy only cured poison but didn't heal you, sage would cure poison and fill up your entire health. This is used similarly to how palo santo is burned. For this you would let it get a little more aflame because typically the areas are bigger when using sage. Just like a rare potion, you use sage when the event calls for it, or if you just don't have any other remedy potions in your inventory.

Let's take a pause here really quickly to understand how to activate these potions. If this were a video game, you would consume the potions. In the game of life, we obviously,

DON'T CONSUME THE POTIONS.

We activate them. I was advised to write that, so it was clear. I don't need any lawsuits here. How do we activate incense, palo santo and sage for the most effectiveness?

Let's jump into the LTUVG app for today's mission and I will show you!

CLEANSING TOOL 1 - SMUDGING, NATURE'S REMEDY

Cleansing Tools 1:

Smudging, Natures Remedy Unlocked
Go to LTUVG App

Similar to food consumption, it's also important to buy ethically sourced sage and palo santo, as their harvesting can be done unconsciously. A general rule, if it doesn't say it's ethically sourced and is produced in the US, it probably is NOT ethically sourced. Now let's move onto the heavy hitter cleansing agents. The Mr. Clean and Magic eraser of the remedy potions.

Legendary Remedy Potion - Salt: The Cleanse-All for remedy potions, and Ward. Salt, especially sea or Himalayan salt, is a potent cleanser and has warding abilities for keeping negative energy out. It's like curing your character of all ailments with an additional +5 constitution to ward off other negative effects. Zai and I had to use this as we were escaping Mordor to protect us. IT WORKS. Since we are constantly working with energy in our work, we cleanse with salt daily, keeping a little pitcher and container of pink salt near in the shower. If you are an empath, I HIGHLY recommend this. It's a straightforward way to feel 20-30 percent better, maybe even more depending on your line of work. If you interact with a lot of people during the day, incorporating this in your practice will change your life. Epsom salt baths are also beneficial if you are feeling depressed, sick, or lethargic in the body.

Mythic Remedy Potion - Copal/Resin: The Cure-All for remedy potions. A resin derived from tree sap; this centuries-old tool is like your Magic Eraser of spiritual cleansing agents. This would be the potion that cleansed all status ailments and healed your party. In real-life terms, this removes day- or weeks-old negative energy stuck to you or a loved one. For plant medicine ceremonies, this is what shamans use to remove any negative energy being released.

Outside of a ceremony, let's say you and your spouse or sibling had a big fight where some heavy words and hurtful things were said. I highly recommend using sage and palo santo if you don't have this resin on you. But at a minimum, having some authentically sourced copal resin incense sticks can also do a world of good. Etsy typically has some good authentic resources, and again, if you have any questions, please comment on the appropriate Guild Channels so it gets answered ASAP.

I know you are probably wondering how effective these cleansing agents are. I want to share what I saw with my own eyes- it immediately improved the life of a plant. This story changed my view on the importance of cleansing forever.

BACK TO MORDOR

So, after Zai'Ra and I were engaged, we went back to do another ceremony with Shar. Our first ceremonies with her and Kanna had allowed us to connect on an even deeper soul level with ourselves, and we wanted to bring this magic to our friends and family. As mentioned earlier, while Shar was living in her purpose, she also needed a lot of financial help—like many individuals at the time. Her film production business had gone under, and she asked for our support. At the time, we were so inspired by her and the magic of Kanna that we wanted to dive into being in service with her. We wanted to make the world a better place, one healed person at a time.

For anyone concerned about the safety of the individuals who were in ceremony with us, we took precautions and required proof of a negative covid test before each retreat. Not one person ever contracted COVID, and we are grateful for this Divine protection.

One morning in the fall of 2020, after an intense one-on-one ceremony, we were cleaning and noticed one of our plants, a new pothos, was wilting! Pothos are very resilient, they don't require much water or sunlight, and this one was young and spry the day before. Pothos are also air cleansers by absorbing pollutants. We immediately knew it must have absorbed the trauma that was released the night before! We lit some sage and started smudging and didn't see a change in the plant.

Shar saw Zai and I working on the plant, and she lit a charcoal and came sauntering over with a smirk on her face. Once she got to us, she sprinkled some copal resin on the charcoal, and to our amazement, the pothos literally sprang back to life! I wish I had a video of this, because it was instantaneous. As the smoke of the copal rose between the many leaves of the pothos, you could see the limbs of the plant immediately rise, almost as if we were bending it upward with our fingers. Once the pothos was back to its healthy self, Shar smiled, gave us a wink, and waltzed back to her room.

Let this be a lesson to you. The next time you are in an emotional funk and can't pull yourself out of it, find some sage or palo santo, and if that doesn't work, copal yourself! Until you experience the sudden shift yourself, you won't truly appreciate it, so try it. What do you have to lose? And once you have an experience, feel free to share it in the "Real Life Wins!" Channel

CLEANSING TOOL 2 - SALF OF THE EARTH

For those who are allergic to smoke, prefer to work with water, or need deeper energetic cleansing, jump back into the LTUVG app to access your second tier of energetic remedy potions.

Cleansing Tool 2:

Salt of the Earth Unlocked
Go to LTUVG App

I promise that these cleansing tools will change not just how you feel, but also how you move through your day with more energy. Try this consistently over a one-, two-, and four-week period, and let the community know your results in the "Gratitude Lobby" Channel! Your experiences will help others live their best lives. The more XP gained, the more the entire community benefits. Remember, we are in this together.

Next, we are going to tap into more dormant superhuman abilities so that you can get one step closer to rescuing your inner child waiting for you.

Level 4 Recap:

- Items Slots Unlocked
  - Incense
  - Palo Santo
  - Sage
  - Salt (Himalayan)
  - Copal/Resin
- Universal Tools Acquired
  - Smudging
  - Self-Cleansing Spell
  - Salt Rinse Spell

LEVEL 5

UNIVERSAL PRINCIPLES OF THE GAME OF LIFE

MOORE ON THE HOLOGRAPHIC UNIVERSE THEORY

Let's think about the holographic universe in another way. About seven years ago, a NASA scientist wrote an article that said he believed that we lived in a holographic universe.[51] This is coming from someone who studies the earth and outer space for a living. Edgar Mitchell is another NASA astronaut with solid evidence supporting this theory.[52] The majority of us are not rocket scientists, so I'll give you the CliffsNotes version.

The scientist referred to something called Moore's Law, which effectively states that computing power doubles every couple of years. Technically it states that the

[51] Collier, J. (2017). "The Holographic Principle." NASA Technical Reports Server.
[52] Mitchell, E. (1996). "The Way of the Explorer: An Apollo Astronaut's Journey Through the Material and Mystical Worlds."

number of transistors on an integrated circuit will double every one to two years with minimal rise in cost, which is what determines the computing power. As of the time of the paper, supercomputers were operating at double the speed of the "measured" human brain, and by now, these supercomputers can compute every thought a person would have in an 80-year lifetime in the span of a month.[53] Now let's look at human behavior. We are pushing forward with AI and augmented reality, with Apple Vision, considering profits over consequences. There are some crazy things AI is doing, including helping me reference this book, and it's only going to exponentially increase in the next two, five, ten, twenty, fifty years and beyond. As the line in *Jurassic Park* goes,

"We are so caught up with 'if we can' that we don't stop to think, 'should we'."

Dr. Terrile, an astronomer and director of the Center for Evolutionary Computation and Automated Design and NASA's Jet Propulsion Lab, believes that the holographic simulation hypothesis has "beautiful and profound" implications. For if we follow this trajectory, we will soon be able to create our own simulations where we all are operating in a shared world. Take that a step further—how would you treat your world if you

---

[53] Solon, O. (2016). "Is our world a simulation? Why some scientists say it's more likely than not." The Guardian.
https://www.theguardian.com/technology/2016/oct/11/simulated-world-elon-musk-the-matrix

BELIEVED that to be true? I know what I would do, I would want to know all the ins and outs of the simulation, how to play it, how to maximize my experience, how to help others do the same.

Your turn. Ground your feet, take a couple deep breaths in, box breathing if you feel called. Close your eyes, and ask yourself,

"What would I do if I lived in a holographic universe?"

Okay, you're back, how do you feel? What would you do? You know someone else who believes we live in a holographic universe? Elon Musk. He famously said, "If you assume any rate of improvement at all, games will eventually be indistinguishable," concluding "that it's most likely we're in a simulation." Believing this, how has Musk decided to play life? I'm **not** a Musk fan, to be clear, but I am impressed by how much he's pushed the bounds of this reality. With Tesla, solar energy and self-guiding rockets that launch into space and return. As a result, his company is on the forefront of exploration.

He is tapping into imagination abilities to manifest the creations in his mind. Is he doing it for the better good or his own good? I'll leave that up to higher powers to decide. What you have control over is how you will use your own imagination. Will you use it for the good of everyone involved, including yourself? Or just for yourself? It's up to you.

Speaking of choice, let's choose to embrace the possibility that we indeed are in a realistic video game, in which we CHOSE to enter. If you haven't seen the movie *Soul*, it's a must-watch. In it, it talks about the "great forgetting," a process by which we, as souls, had a plan for how we wanted to experience earth. We didn't have a roadmap, but we had checkpoints that we wanted to hit. We just had to forget them to come to earth, because part of life is walking the path to our goals. It's the journey that helps define our experience, not just our arrival.

Imagine if you started a game and already had all the skills and abilities from the very beginning. The bosses were all easy and the story predictable the entire way to the final boss. You saw your pathway so clearly that there was no mystery. Pretty boring game if you ask me.

So why would we want life to be easy? Instead, if we radically accept life as it is, we can focus on how to overcome the obstacles and create our desired life. I've experienced death, pain, poverty and suffering, as you might have. So, I don't say this lightly. I say it with a ton of reverence. Reverence for my tumultuous life that has, through pain and suffering, taught me so much about beauty, perseverance, laughter, joy, and unconditional love.

"Unconditional love is the greatest gift we can give. It is the energy that holds the Universe together."

Trappist monk Thomas Keating taught this[54], and I've felt it in my life over and over. I believe that it's a big reason we are here on this Earth - to remember the power of unconditional love. So, let's continue remembering.

THE 6CS OF UNIVERSAL PRINCIPLES

There are six Universal Principles in the game of life, with a seventh that holds them all together. The overarching principle of this journey to rescue your inner child is to be like a child. To be curious, with all of the experiences and lessons you receive on this adventure. As the saying goes,

"What you resist, persists."

And if you want to grow exponentially in your powers, be aware of areas of resistance. Those are the doors to your biggest powers. Negative self-talk, doubt, saying "I'll do this exercise tomorrow" or "I'm not comfortable with that", those are indications that that is EXACTLY where you need to lean in, with <u>curiosity</u>. If a caterpillar was afraid to push against the cocoon because it made it feel uncomfortable, then it would never emerge as a beautiful butterfly. If Link didn't want to explore the unknown mountains and lands around him, then he would never find those incredibly powerful swords, shields, and gems that helped to increase his health so

---

[54] Keating, T. (1999). "Open Mind, Open Heart: The Contemplative Dimension of the Gospel."

he could eventually take on Gannon and rescue Princess Zelda.

Do you want to get to the final boss with scrappy items and a little bit of experience points because you were afraid of the hard quests along the way? If you're this far in the book, I know that you are ready to explore your inner world fully. Remembering is a lifetime experience, so we aren't in a rush, but these principles are something new to practice, and every one of these also levels up your V.I.S.A. level. This will allow you to grind as much as you want, earn as much XP as possible, and gain those GOUs that might RNG (random number generate) into a soul shard!

When you approach a world boss, it's more fun than challenging. It will be difficult, requiring all your Universal Attributes, tools, learned practices and more. Lean into each challenge with curiosity, trusting that if it makes you uncomfortable, then there will be a bigger reward on the other side of that challenge. What is it? Only you will find out, but I guarantee that it will serve you in your quest to reclaim aspects of yourself and eventually, your inner child.

The other six C's of Universal Principles we will cover are: Consistency, Compassion, Clarity, Creativity, Courage, and Conviction. Each of these Cs, as we go through them, will conclude with another unlocked skill (or skills) to support you on your journey. But first, let's connect with a meditation so that we can remember how to play within our own mind.

QUEST 11 – PLAY!

One thing that we've forgotten to do as adults is to play more often. Not necessarily playing outwards, there are tons of people who play video games, over three billion, I believe. But how many of y'all have a practice of playing with your own imagination? Of playing with your thoughts? If you are like the average person, your thoughts are pre-programmed with fears, anxiety, to-do lists, worries. As we previously covered, on average many of our thoughts are repetitive and negative, although you've been working to shift that since we started this book. Today's meditation takes another step in that direction with a fun exercise that will activate our first gaming simulation in our Imagination Realization Station. This game will begin to break down negative thought loops with fun to rewire our brain. Why do we want to rewire our brain? Because of this simple fact about how our brains are wired in the first place.

Neurons that fire together wire together.

Our brains are composed of billions of neurons that communicate through synaptic connections. With every thought and experience, the neurons in our brain are trained to either build on the things that keep us safe and/or we enjoy, or to redirect energy from areas that put us in perceived danger and/or we don't enjoy. When we repeatedly think the same thoughts, these neurons form strong connections, making it easier for those thoughts to occur again in the future. Through repetition, thoughts become actions, actions become habits, habits become beliefs, beliefs become a part of our personality, a part of who we are.

This begs the question, if many of us have spent years, maybe decades, thinking and doing the same things day in and day out, how does one hope to unwind these neural networks? We need to disrupt the automatic firing of these neural pathways to change these patterns. To accomplish this, we will play a little game called metacognition. Metacognition is a state where you can think about your thoughts. It gives us the ability to observe our thought patterns, so that if there is one that we know hurts our ability to accomplish our goals, we can reprogram it with a positive thought instead.

Similar to creative mode in *Minecraft*, your thoughts, conscious and subconscious, are the building blocks of the habits and beliefs that make up your mind. When in survival mode, you don't have time to be the observer, you are building with the limitations of whatever world you are in. In life, when you aren't meditating, the limitations that you've put on yourself and your YOUniverse keep you from breaking out of your old patterns. It is possible to break out of them in real time, but it's much easier to do in the meditation space first. But don't worry, we will cover more strategies on habit building in the upcoming quests in this book.

In this meditation, we are going to take advantage of our imagination and its ability to create any scenario we can visualize.

Did you play platform games like *Super Mario* or *Crash Bandicoot*? Where your goal would be to effectively run and jump from platform to platform while not getting caught by the baddies or obstacles that were on each platform? Let's play a version of that in our minds.

MISSION 11: CLOUD JUMPING PROGRAM

This next mission is a fun one! It's our first attempt at an active meditation within your subconscious. We are going to begin to interact with our thoughts and attempt to clear them as if we were playing a platform game like Super Mario.

So grab your LTUVG app and let's "jump" in! *ya, wah, whoooooo!*

Mission 11 Activated

Open the LTUVG App and access Mission 11: *Cloud Jumping Program*

In this chapter, we've explored how our actions create habits, but it's crucial to remember that these habits can be broken by disrupting the chain of thought patterns that fire together. Meditation, particularly the Cloud Jumping Program, is a powerful tool to level up your Awareness attribute. Remember, there is only one way forward, and that is up.

Don't take yourself so seriously.

Say that to yourself a few times, write it down, soften yourself, and watch the world soften around you. Have fun! The Cloud Jumping Program is a playful game to practice presence anytime, anywhere. Especially try this for a few minutes if you ever find yourself in an area in or near nature that just feels special.

Level 5 Recap:

- <u>Subtle Energy XP/Grinding Activities</u>
    - Cloud Jumping Program

LEVEL 6

HARD WORK DOESN'T BEAT CONSISTENCY

I once was a talented wide receiver for a Princeton football team who never saw the playing field. I was fast, strong, hard to tackle, had amazing hands, and nobody outworked me on the field or in the gym. Unless I was late and arrogant about it. I was what one might call, "uncoachable." I don't have many regrets in life, but this was one I held for a long time. I would have dreams years after college when I was back at Princeton - I didn't know the playbook and was worried about being put in. It took me many ceremonies to reach a place of peace for this part of my life. I eventually came to be grateful for it. The pain of not fulfilling a football career in this life was necessary for me to accept humility in responsibility.

The most invaluable lesson I learned from this moment was that no matter how much talent I had, being reliable and consistent trumps talent every time.

If you are talented but can't get out of your own way to be there for the people who are relying on you, then it's almost worse! Because it's "wasted potential." The kicker is that it hurts me more than it hurts the team! My senior year we would win a championship, and I had no contribution to it. Instead, I rode the bench for my career. Again, I am grateful, because the challenges I created for myself led to me discovering Reiki, humbling myself, and when I almost lost it all on that motorcycle, it taught me to:

"Let go of my own Unique Skills, so that I could level up my Universal skills."

Although I wouldn't have worded it that way at the time, this experience allowed me to understand the first Universal Principle, Consistency.

This relates directly to our previous analysis of the compounding interest of just getting 1 percent better every day. Remember, after one year of getting 1 percent better every day, you will be collecting roughly 37 times more XP, a 37x multiplier! In two years, you will have a 1400x multiplier for XP earned daily. You'll be 1400 times better at activating your imagination, tapping into the subtle energy realm, and leveling up your life. It's why all of the most successful CEOs include Consistently waking up early and having daily routines as a part of their must have principles of life.[55]

Just as my lack of consistency held me back from accomplishing my football dreams, you will need to apply consistency to the practices you are learning in this book to collect your daily experience points and maintain your XP multiplier. Taking a day off will only slow your progress. Even if you just practice for five minutes, you'll maintain and increase your multiplier, leveling up your life in the process.

I like to think of daily practices as "grinding" for experience points in your favorite RPG or mobile game. If you are not familiar with the term, grinding is the process of engaging in repetitive tasks to gain XP to improve your abilities and unlock new skills. Grinding is essential for leveling up so that we can overcome the biggest challenges in any game, including life. Every time we sit with a practice, we get a daily bonus of experience points just for engaging with this practice. For anyone who played *Destiny*, *WoW*, or *any gacha game*, every day you logged in you had a list of missions to do that would give you a large boost of experience.

Think of each practice you are learning as one of these daily missions. Each practice is designed to give a boost to a specific attribute or skill tree simply by doing it consistently. As a benefit, the more consecutive you complete these exercises, the more XP bonuses you

---

[55] Panda, A., Jain, N. K., Nambudiri, R., & Garg, S. (2021). "The relationship between CEO personality and company performance: An empirical study of S&P 500 companies." Business Perspectives and Research, 9(1), 76-91.

receive! And if you haven't unlocked the bonus Mission 10 yet, where you get a galactic compass to know which skills will benefit you each day, I highly recommend attempting that mission soon.

This wouldn't be a good inspiration manual if it didn't inspire you to be creative in your healing adventure. What do I mean by this? I'm here to give you some tips, some "bio hacks" and mind-hacks, whereby you can utilize your enjoyment of video games to reframe what building daily practices feels like.

There is an amazing author and speaker, James Clear, who wrote a book called *Atomic Habits*. Pretty dope name, and also full of incredible ways to improve our habits, but the biggest thing is to just take that first step. It could mean that daily meditation for you starts with three to five box breaths and then expands from there as you feel the benefits in your life. He referred to it as "getting 1 percent better every day," sound familiar? Haha.

Okay, so the tip that you haven't heard before (unless you've read *Atomic Habits*) is a concept called habit stacking.

It utilizes the fact that stopping old habits is hard,
To balance out the concept that good habits
are hard to start.

What do I mean? Meaning that you place a new habit that you want to start, after a habit that you already have. Let's say that you have a habit of unwinding with a video game after work or maybe in the morning on the weekend, ohhhhh, I know, after a long week of work. Sound familiar? Me too.

While I was climbing up the ladder of success in NYC, I couldn't wait to get home on Friday and play *Final Fantasy* for hours, completing all the side quests and special weapon quests. I miss those days, but I'm looking forward to when this book is in your hands, and I'm able to play it. It will make the reward that much sweeter.

Depending on when you are reading this, it might be happening right now. That example isn't what habit stacking is though. Habit stacking helps you accomplish your goals through building off of a habit you already have. Habit combos I like to call them.

As an example, let's say I drink a cup of coffee every morning to get going. To create an easy habit combo, I agree to do breathwork for five minutes as I wait for my coffee to brew. Or you can do it after the coffee is made, while it cools down. This way you start a habit and also giving yourself a reward. This brings up another important concept, what is a habit in the first place?

In its basic form, a habit is the strategy we follow to solve the problems we repeatedly face in life. Every time we repeat the actions of our habits, it gives them more and more XP. But we only have a finite number of XP we can earn and allocate during our lives. Many of them are probably wrapped up in our Unique Attributes skill trees. Sadly, we don't have a way to transfer those XP overnight, but if you get at least 1 percent better every day, you'll be in a completely new world in a year, and a new universe in two years. I'm four years in and I've already been blessed to raise millions of dollars to support and grow the causes that are near and dear to Zai'Ra and my heart. I want this future for you, and habit combos are an amazing life hack to help get you there.

So, habits are these strategies, and we need to understand how these systems are built so that we can find points of weakness. If a bad habit were a mini-boss, once understood, it could then be used to support your journey of mastering life. If you played *Zelda*, much like being able to turn the sentinels back on your side by defeating the souls trapped within them, this is what we can do with our habits. There are four weak points, or steps, within creating habits. When you see them, it's an opportunity to raise our awareness and remind ourselves of the good habits we are setting for ourselves. These four steps are the following:

1. **Cue**: This is the trigger that tells your brain to initiate the habit. For example, it could be a phone banner pop-up to remind you to check an app or the smell of delicious cookies.
   Gaming Analogy: Think of it as the in-game alert of a public mission that just popped up on the MMORPG you are playing.
2. **Craving**: This is the desire for the specific outcome. Which would be your desire to know the message that was sent in the app, or your desire to eat the cookie and taste how good it is.
   Gaming Analogy: It's your desire to get the XP bonus for completing the public mission and

possibly getting an engram (think Gem of Understanding).

3. **Response:** This is the thought or action you take to satisfy the craving. This might be opening the app or eating the cookie.
   Gaming Analogy: It's you staying up another fifteen minutes to complete this public mission, running across the game to get to the area before the boss is defeated.
4. **Reward:** This is the payoff you get from satisfying the craving. In real life, it's the satisfaction of seeing the message or tasting the cookie.
   Gaming Analogy: Plain and simple, how many XP did you get and what dope item did you get? Can you use the money you earned to buy anything new?

At each point of this process, there is something going on under the surface that is acting like a carrot pulling the rabbit, or the dog chasing the fake rabbit. It's called a hormone, or neurotransmitter, which is released by the brain to tell the body "this is enjoyable." This neurotransmitter is primarily dopamine. It works in our favor if the action truly benefits us, or if it just satisfies a craving it can leave us unbalanced and craving even more afterwards.

Think of dopamine as the XP multiplier in whatever action you are pursuing and the craving that you are attempting to satisfy. When you complete the action, this multiplier massively determines how many XP you get. Usually if the level you are completing is difficult, the rewards will be big. Dopamine is a response to the XP multiplier when you get the reward in the habit loop.

The habit being formed could range from being trivial to life preserving, and in gaming, the body responds the same biologically. If it's trivial like checking social media notifications, it might be a small XP multiplier habit, you're not expecting much, but if it's completely a public event, then it'll be higher because it's drawing you to invest more of your time and energy.

Here is an example of what literally happens to our dopamine levels at each stage of habit creation:

1. **Cue Phase**: The game alert for the public event pops up. You get a slight bump in dopamine levels. This is the carrot at the end of the stick, motivating you to move forward, believing that by doing this activity, you'll get more XP faster. Saving you time and energy.
2. **Craving Phase**: You run to the location, only to find a huge boss there. This is going to be difficult. Your dopamine level drops below baseline, creating a sense of urgency. You are feeling the pressure to satisfy this craving.
3. **Response Phase**: You begin fighting and collectively defeat the boss! Your dopamine level starts to anticipate victory close at hand.
4. **Reward Phase**: What did you get? If the XP bonus and items are on par with the challenge, then your dopamine will spike at a normal range. But if the XP bonus is higher, like a lot higher,

> then your dopamine will spike above normal range. Resulting in the desire to play another Public Quest! And if the XP bonus is a dud, then your dopamine levels will also dud, and you might NEED another Public Quest in order to get your dopamine hit. The measure of the difference between what you expected the XP bonus to be and what it really was is called Reward Prediction Error.

See how the cycle continues? Good video games know EXACTLY how to tap into this system to keep you playing their games. The reason I'm interweaving these concepts together is so that you can use it to get better at REAL LIFE, instead of just video games.

Perfect, we have our four awareness points of habit forming, as well as what is happening mentally and physiologically. Let's form our plan of activation to change these habits.

With compassion, let me ask you:

Have you ever felt that the world
has leveled up around you,
But you haven't leveled up with it?

If this is something you've ever felt, it isn't your fault. I repeat, it's not your fault. It wasn't my fault either, but it did need to happen. What's important about acknowledging this feeling, as small as it might be, is that it's also a blessing that we can be here now, and in this moment, level ourselves up together.

Through the quests, missions, practices and activities in this inspiration manual, we can upgrade our lives so we can enjoy the beauty of the world around us. If new habits are hard, and you are already here, then start by reading five to ten pages a day. Remember the promise you made to start the book, and the consequence and reward you promised yourself.

One hack that I've adopted is to add a new activity after something I already do as a habit, or "habit stack." For example, with breathwork, if you still struggle to do it 3 times a day, just try doing it one time a day after breakfast, coffee, or brushing your teeth. After that is well established and you see the benefits of doing this consistently, then you can add another session at the end of the day, after the commute home, or before you game to unwind from a long day, start with breathwork, and it will also provide more focus for your gaming session.

This method has been a tried-and-true way for me to be successful in my life. It made things I used to not enjoy much more fun. This book wouldn't be here without this method, that's for sure.

Have you ever had a friend who wrote a book? It becomes this thing that takes on a life of its own. Once you start telling your friends, many of them will start an internal clock. A year, two, or more may go by and the friends stop paying attention when you say, "I'm writing a book." This process started in February of last year, with a thirty-day book writing challenge. It was an amazing product. I wrote most of the rough draft in thirty days. The last 30 percent would take another two months, finishing it as I touched down from a fourteen-hour flight from Tokyo back to Atlanta for my fortieth birthday. Then it became static.

To be completely honest, I had resistance to the editing phase. The method I used relied solely on being "in flow," connected to my higher self. This methodology allowed me to channel the book creatively. Afterward, the analytical mind is needed to shape and mold the creation. It was in this stage that I began to procrastinate.

I started playing a video game that is a lot of fun, challenging, and magic—*Magic the Gathering (MTG): Arena*. If you are not familiar with it, it's a competitive magic card game, where you use mana to build up your energy to cast spells that can be creatures, buffs, debuffs, enchantments, etc., with the intention of taking your opponent's life to zero. After a long day of working my day job and then building up my online business or doing retreat planning for our nonprofit, I would binge play *MTG: Arena*. One night, after being up until 3 a.m. before a big test for my Breath Masters Certificate, I told myself, this is enough.

It also was that during the breathwork session, I received a very clear message and vision from my experience.

Gaming in the realm of MTG was taking XP away from the Game of Real Life.

And I needed this XP to go towards all of the other things I was trying to accomplish. A book doesn't just give birth to itself, you have to push yourself to bring it into the world. I reminded myself of the promise I made, got re-energized, and started reading *Atomic Habits*. I needed my own motivation to keep going, and in discovering this motivation, I saw another way to also help you all develop good habits so you too can earn more experience points and accomplish your dreams in a shorter amount of time with more ease!

Through James Clear's book, I learned that I could use habit stacking to motivate me as well as regulate my dopamine at the same time! I made a rule that I would have to edit ten pages before I could play one to three games of *MTG* afterwards. This technically is a new ability for you RPG buffs, we have Cantrips! The first one I taught you was **Habit Stacking**. The next one is **Reverse Habit Stacking**, which is just doing the habit you want to establish BEFORE an already established habit. For those unfamiliar with Cantrips, in any video game RPG, they are skills that you can use that may be magical in nature but not cost any mana to cast. It still takes up a turn, but they also can be used to augment your special abilities. For more information on these, go check out Cantrips Videos in the "Resources" tab in the Life Gamers Guild community section of the app.

These two tools you can use in any situation as much as you need. In my case, I chose to use my desire to play *MTG: Arena*, the craving, to inspire a response to edit pages in this book. Such that the promise of playing (and winning) a match in *MTG* fed me enough dopamine to keep me coming back to editing the book! Problem solved! Not yet.

Soon I was playing more than one game after I edited ten pages. Especially if I lost, I'd want to play again, and again, and...raise your hand if you are familiar with this story. What was the result? I'd lose any momentum editing the book because I was diverting more energy to playing *MTG* than editing the book. The dopamine hit from playing *MTG* was too big to bring me back to writing the book, which only provided a small hit of dopamine.

I thought I was giving myself proper dopamine, but really what I was doing was giving myself "unearned dopamine." Unearned dopamine is one of the biggest killers of starting good habits.

Unearned Dopamine is earned when your task is just motion, But it doesn't get you closer to your goals.

As a colleague once said, "Don't confuse action with accomplishment," referring to making sure your actions have intention behind them, otherwise it's just doing for the sake of doing. I would only correct that by saying that sometimes you need to get in motion to understand the meaning behind the action. This was the case for me, and I actually recommend it to you. We all have to learn, and sometimes baby steps help us activate our own inspiration and imagination.

Try adding one of these activities right before you usually play a game. Just five to ten minutes to start. It can be breathwork, visualization, something simple and easy to do. If it's in the same area you game in, you can even light some palo santo or sage and set an intention for your gaming practice (real life and on the TV). What you'll find is that you'll start to improve your focus for the game you play afterward. The experience is more present with you. I noticed this when I was playing *MTG*, which is a very technical game. I got up to diamond league multiple times, and the best games I had were after I did breathwork and was grounded.

As you game, like me, you might start to realize that there are other passions you have. Or that the skills you are building through improving your Imagination Realization Realm are bringing you more wealth, improving your health, relationships, and ability to flow through life with more ease. You will naturally want to practice these abilities and build up your V.I.S.A. on your own. I eventually decided to go all in with finishing this book and since I made that decision, I have logged zero minutes of *MTG: Arena*.

Now, what five-minute breathwork exercise is there that can be the Trojan horse of building this habit up? It's part of the 3/6/5 Method, **Level 2 Co-Breath**.

We are leveling up one of the first skills we practiced, coherent breathing. This time, since our imagination is leveled up more, we are going to add visualization to our Co-Breath to activate our heart with it. Let's learn how to integrate the lungs, mind, and heart together in this next quest and gain some more GOUs!

QUEST 12 - 365 ALLOWS YOU TO THRIVE

We want to be consistent. We want to establish practices that we do every day for a week, then a month, then multiple months, and then years in a row.

It's been difficult, but every day, regardless of whether I'm enjoying nature with Zai'Ra and our cats, or I am moving through a tragedy like the passing of my cousin who left behind four young children, I have nothing but gratitude in my heart for the life I have. That is true freedom, and this 3/6/5 method can play a huge part in helping you accomplish the same thing.

So, open the LTUVG app and head to Mission 12.

MISSION 12: UPLEVELING YOUR CO-BREATH

Mission 12 Activated
Open the LTUVG App and access Mission 12:
Upleveling Your Co-Breath

Amazing! You've just leveled up your first skill! (*Spoiler Alert: more will be coming)* How do you feel?

Make sure to journal for five minutes to connect with any messages your subconscious might want to share about the experience. What did you visualize? What brought you peace? How can you bring that peace of presence into your day today?

Remember, your breath is your ability to control yourself in the Game of Life with more consistency and ease. If you ever feel yourself getting angry or into a fight or flight mode during the day, check in with the breath and practice your Level 2 Co-Breath. With practice you'll be able to tap into your higher self on the fly to understand how to best apply your gifts to the situation at hand; entering HUD mode so you can collect those GOUs!

QUEST 13 - BUILDING ON OUR BREATHWORK

We have our breathwork tool, so that no matter what emotion we are feeling, we can simply change our breathing pattern and become less angry, less stressed, and see what we are supposed to learn from each situation. At a minimum, it can help us surrender to the moment and be more present. But why is "being present" so important? Well, let's look at how the present moment works in a video game.

In any video game, how do you gain more experience points? When are you able to actually affect change in the game? Only in the present moment of the game. If the game is paused, you can't actually play the game, even entering into creator mode in *Minecraft*, the game has to be moving in real time for you to earn experience in the game. Life is very much the same, in that the only moment that you can affect change is in the present moment.

What if you just accepted the flow of life, like you accept the flow of the video games you play? Focusing on the best way to overcome the task at hand instead of being frustrated that there is a challenge in the first place? Even surrendering, in the spiritual sense, doesn't mean to give in. No. When I say "surrender," it simply means:

Accepting that your way may not be the best approach to a situation.

Isn't this how we game? Flow with the rules of the game to create the best outcome for ourselves. Or at least we have fun doing it. We are curious about the pathway, trusting that it will guide us to our intended destination, if we just let it. The more present we are in any moment, the more aware we are of employing our abilities to transmute these experiences into the best outcome for ourselves and everyone involved. Here are the signs of being ultimately present:

1. Breathing controlled and composed
2. Being aware of our emotions
3. Being non-reactionary
4. Being an observer of your surroundings until action is needed
5. If in a conversation, you are actively listening, asking more than telling

Qualitatively, these are questions you can ask yourself if/when you feel like you are present.

How is it making you feel?
What elements are involved?

How can I move from the feeling I have now to a feeling of gratitude?

If this is your first time trying to ask these questions, then we are going to need to practice this when we aren't in a real-life situation. This is where meditation comes in handy.

To help with that, just as we upgraded your Co-Breath, we are going to level up your visualization abilities with a Level 2 Awareness Meditation. The name is going to change, and this will be one of your most used abilities until it becomes second nature. It's called the Heart-Mind Centering (HMC) Technique.

MISSION 13: LEVELING UP! THE HEART-MIND CENTERING TECHNIQUE

A couple of years ago, I was searching for a way to help others activate their intuition and improve their meditation skills at a beginner level. Something that is easy and straightforward. What did the Universe bring me? It's called the Silva Ultramind Method. What got me to believe in something that sounded like a secret government program from Marvel comics? You'll find this compelling story in the next mission in the LTUVG app.

Mission 13 Activated
Open the LTUVG App and access Mission 13:
Leveling Up! The HMC Technique

Amazing work! You now are equipped with your Level 2 Awareness Activity. I love this as a main meditation because it isn't too "woo-woo." I have no issue with things that are "woo-woo," but I am also aware that for many who are new to the metaphysical world, the more practical and straightforward it is, the more accessible it is. This exercise is great because it allows you to grind every day to improve all skill trees of your V.I.S.A. And the more consistent you are, that also improves your Consistency skill tree!

I did this exercise consistently for months before I leveled it up even further, decreasing the time I needed to drop into the alpha/theta brain wave mode, eventually being able to do it simply by counting from three to one.

This is your grinding tool that will level up your V.I.S.A. most efficiently right now, so make it your best friend. Habit combo it with your level 2 Co-Breath or another activity you do in the morning, and it will pay dividends just like it did for Vishen. Who knows, you might become the next millionaire from doing this method. Just make sure to let the community know when you do!

BONUS QUEST 14 - YOUR MULTIDIMENSIONAL IMAX THEATER

Yesterday, you learned how to center yourself and program yourself with a positive mantra. If you feel confident in your ability to tap into this skill, we are going to give your ESC button another technique. To do so, you're going to lean into your imagination and use a little trick with your focus to activate a special gland in the body that has been utilized by ancient civilizations dating back to and beyond the Egyptians.

What is it about breathwork that magnifies our ability to tap into our superpowers? On a physiological level, breath helps us release the toxins in our body. Nearly 70 percent of the toxins in our body are released through our breath and our lymphatic system.[56] This is why deep breaths into our belly are so important for us. If we aren't breathing fully, then it's putting extra workload on our other detoxifying organs, forcing them to work overtime to detoxify the rest of our body.

Breath also cycles something else throughout the body. A liquid that encapsulates and protects your brain and spinal cord called cerebral spinal fluid (CSF). Think of it like the fluid that holds Metroid in her healing chamber or the fluid that holds Goku in the healing chamber after he got obliterated by Frieza. It nourishes your brain and nerves as it acts like the superspeed highway that transports the necessary hormones, like dopamine, for you to operate at full capacity. This fluid must get cycled out every day, and this is facilitated by our breath.

Your body cycles it slowly throughout the day, about four times in every 24-hour period. Like an inchworm or a drawstring that comes out of your sweats or sweaters. When you inhale, the body contracts the fluid, and when you exhale, the CSF expands and cycles a tiny bit more

---

56

down the body.[57] Why is this important? It's because we have this special gland in the center of the brain called the pineal gland, and whenever we breathe in or out, and hold our breath, the CSF puts pressure on it.

If you look up twenty degrees and turn your gaze into the center of your head, you are also putting your attention right on the pineal gland (PG). There is this saying:

"Where your focus goes, your energy flows."

Looking up twenty degrees, in the middle of your head, literally puts your focus/energy on your pineal gland while breathing and holding your breath puts a mechanical pressure on it. What happens when we put pressure on this gland? It's literally like our body is an advanced machine because it creates what is called a piezoelectric effect.

The piezoelectric effect is a phenomenon where mechanical pressure or stress is applied to something which then generates an electrical charge. In the case of the pineal gland, there are tiny crystals that, when electrified, turn the PG into a transistor. A transistor is effectively a mechanism that acts as a sender and receiver of messages or frequencies. Studies are still emerging in this field of study, but Dr. Joe Dispenza has done studies with the PG and through experiments and corresponding brain scans, he's shown that "when activated, the PG becomes a conduit for higher-

---

[57] Sakka, L., Coll, G., & Chazal, J. (2011). Anatomy and physiology of cerebrospinal fluid. European Annals of Otorhinolaryngology, Head and Neck Diseases, 128(6), 309-316.

dimensional energies, leading to profound, transcendental experiences."[58] Professor Raj Kumara Sahai published a study in 2014 that corroborated this data as well, along with citing previous experiments showing calcite in the PG, a tell-tale sign of piezoelectric effects.[59]

Why is this important? Because these higher-dimensional energies allow us to access information from the subtle energy realm, increasing access to our intuition and ability to visualize the pathway to our dreams. As our imagination levels up, so does our Imagination Realization Station. If you haven't gathered by now, our IR Stations have their own energy, and the more energy they can hold, the more we can create within it. Effectively, we level up our IR Stations any time we engage with our imagination.

Just imagine, ahem, that your IR has its own grid that you can create in, like a 4-dimensional sandbox. Just like the grid that you create in *Minecraft*, this exists within your imagination. At first, you were only able to create a permission rose with your imagination. But as you've been tapping into your imagination, 1 percent at a time, you've slowly been expanding this imagination realization realm (IRR) more and more. Eventually you'll create more constructs to help support you on the pathway to rescue your inner child. The beauty is it just gets better from here.

---

[58] Dispenza, J. (2017). Becoming Supernatural: How Common People Are Doing the Uncommon. Hay House, Inc.

[59] Arun, P., Sanjana, S., Lakshmi, K. R., & Kumar, M. S. (2013). Pineal gland - A structural and functional enigma. Journal of the Anatomical Society of India, 62(2), 181-187.

In this next activity, you are going to gain the ability to project your IR onto a movie screen, where you will visualize a problem and receive information through your inner knowing on how to solve it. So head to the LTUVG App and navigate to this bonus mission.

MISSION 14: UPGRADING YOUR IMAGINATION REALIZATION STATION!

Mission 14 Activated
Open the LTUVG App and access Mission 14:
Upgrading Your Imagination Realization Station!

How was that experience? I bet you didn't realize that EVERYTHING within you is upgradeable. I'm telling you; the limit is the expanse of your imagination. Give gratitude to yourself, this isn't easy work, and you are crushing it!

Wasn't it fun to finally see your problems as projects and then watch them unfold in a way that can create a possible solution? Now all you need to do is take the first step toward it and see the journey toward that future unfold. It may not turn out exactly as you wanted, which might turn out for the better. Remember to start small, just like habits, because it is also your own belief that it will happen which helps to pull that future to you. Why? Well, because whether we imagine it will or won't happen, we are imagining something, consciously or subconsciously, it doesn't matter. Thoughts are thoughts.

This is why upgrading our IR Station, the virtual gaming console within you, is so important.

Imagination Realization activates your inner knowing.

This is the portal of communication between you and your higher self, who provides you with shortcuts to level up your life.

By engaging your imagination, you tap into a wellspring of inner knowledge and wisdom, allowing you to navigate life's challenges with creativity and confidence, unlocking new levels of personal growth and potential. Above all else, you must be CONSISTENT.

SAVE POINT 3 - ON THE GRIND FOR MORE XP

Remember your pledge to yourself to start this book, remember the consequence and/or reward that you made to yourself and this growing community, and remember the feeling of connecting with your higher self. These are all reminders to keep going. If you only practiced three exercises in this entire book, practicing Level 2 Co-Breath, HMC Technique, and the IRR Technique alone will level up your V.I.S.A. and IR Station enough to transform your life.

Take the next couple of days to practice these abilities, because you'll need a basic command of them to take on the next Level, Compassion is the Key. The purpose of practicing these skills will be simple, to earn more experience with your newfound skills, that way, you can overcome life challenges with them!

While this book is fun, remember that it's just an inspiration manual, to support you living your best life as if it were a video game.

Speaking of support, head to the LTUVG app to access the next Save Point! Here you'll find you've unlocked a NEW skill tree to assess, Consistency! You'll also have the option to retake your V.I.S.A. Skill Assessment if you so choose.

Just as we mentioned in the introduction, if your V.I.S.A. allows you to survive in the subtle energy realm, the 6C's of Universal Principles allow you to THRIVE in this "unseen" realm. And as always, we want to level up every skill tree we have, to be the best possible version of ourselves in the Game of Life.

! Save Point 3: !

On the Grind for More XP Unlocked
Go to LTUVG App

Level 6 Recap:

- Physical XP/Grinding Activities:
    - Level 2 Co-Breath
- Subtle Energy XP/Grinding Activities
    - Heart-Mind Centering Technique
    - Imagination Realization Realm Technique

LEVEL 7

COMPASSION IS THE KEY

When we struggle to do our best, what helps us to get back on track? Despite the misconceived belief that being hard on ourselves builds better behavior, studies actually show that Compassion is the key. This reminds me of a cruel study done, this time not on rats, but on humans. Nobody was hurt, physically, but in this study, "The Doughnut & Candy Study," Dr. McGonigal definitely emotionally tormented some people. She examined how self-compassion influences an individual's ability to maintain healthy habits after experiencing a setback. Here is where the cruelty comes in.

One hundred participants, women who were all on a diet plan, were intentionally put in a situation where they "had" to break their diet. They brought these women into a closed room, and asked them to pick out their favorite doughnut, eat it, and give it a rating. One by one, each woman broke their diet, ate one donut, maybe more, and rated them. They were then split up into two groups.

One group, referred to as the self-compassion group, was taken into a room where they received a message encouraging them to be kind and understanding to themselves. The message emphasized the high rate of people who break their diets, and to forgive themselves, acknowledging they aren't alone in their struggles. The other group, the control, was given no such reminder to be compassionate with themselves. They were just sent into the third room, where they waited for the self-compassion group to arrive. Once the groups were reunited, they were bombarded with more sweets! Both groups were then told that they needed to eat as many different types of candy as they could and rank them best to worst. CRUELTY, I tell you!

The control group really got the brunt of this study, because they ended up eating double what the self-compassion group ate. How did this self-compassion group feel afterward? The results showed they felt twenty-five percent less guilty and had twenty percent more motivation to return to their healthy eating plan than the control group.[60] Dr. McGonigal also did more specific studies to measure the odds of someone returning to a habit when given self-compassion vs the normal guilting we do to ourselves. Out of a study of 200 participants, after being given a doughnut and breaking their diet, 71 percent of the self-compassion

---

[60] McGonigal, K. (2011). *The Willpower Instinct: How Self-Control Works, Why It Matters, and What You Can Do to Get More of It.* Avery.

group resumed their diet vs 49 percent of the self-critical group. Similar to the previous study, 27 percent of the self-compassion group experienced less guilt and shame.

These studies showed intimately how guilt and shame are associated with struggling to maintain good habits, while concepts of compassion—acceptance, forgiveness, and normalization—are critical in maintaining and preserving them long-term. This also correlates to the studies of Dr. David Hawkins that placed shame at the bottom of the energetic emotional scale of consciousness, and acceptance and forgiveness on the higher end.

By acknowledging that setbacks are a natural part of the process—everyone slips up—we are able to forgive ourselves for a setback. This allows us to normalize the experience by reminding ourselves that everyone faces challenges when forming new habits. This normalization releases us from the fear of letting ourselves down again if we, for example, miss a day of reading this book or practicing breathwork. When this happens, remember to follow this pattern:

Acceptance grants forgiveness to normalize the difficulty of developing new habits.

So, we can see how self-compassion is important for supporting our first Universal Principle (Consistency), in helping us to establish new habits. However, compassion goes much deeper than that. Remember the quote from the monk Keating? "Unconditional love is...the energy that holds the Universe together?" Well, compassion is unconditional love in action. To give context to the power of unconditional love, I'm going to share an incredibly painful, yet beautiful story of compassion.

QUEST 15 - SACRED HEART JOURNEY

My aunt, who helped raise me during my childhood, became my best friend as I grew into adulthood. Anytime I had issues I couldn't take to my parents; I would lean on her for advice. This was especially true for my family traumas. As an adult, whenever I traveled to Los Angeles, she was the first person I would see. We'd roll one up and share our hearts over a glass or two of Don Julio.

In a family where emotions weren't always received openly, she was a safe haven for my healing process. I also got to learn of the impossible childhood she had, which continued in raising her only son who developed signs of CTE after a truncated NFL football career that had high hopes. I guess you could say we were each other's safe haven. A sacred kinship.

After I visited her in 2015, she received some very tough news. Her doctor had advised her that she would need to go on meds soon because her kidneys were failing her. She was told to change her diet in order to have any chance of avoiding a transplant. After our last visit together, finishing her glass of tequila, she said, "No more Don Julio." She then put herself on a strict heath regimen with hope that future blood tests would come back positively. Simultaneously, my aunt had to move her son in with her because his mental health was deteriorating.

Unfortunately, our mental health laws are not supportive of getting people the help they need without condemning them to a mental health facility. Without being admitted, he would need to be willing to voluntarily take his medication. The only other option was for his mom to call the police on him and have him labeled a "danger" to society. As a black man in Los Angeles, especially during the times of Trayvon Martin and the many others who have lost their lives, this was not an option for my aunt. Instead, she brought him into her garage to live in after she discovered that he was playing chicken with buses and got clipped by one.

Months later, in what would be the last conversation I would have with her, she called with amazing news. Her diet had worked, her health was improving, and she wouldn't need surgery if things continued on that path.

"I have a new lease on life, I'm going to start the business I've always wanted to!"

She shared her news with excitement! Her son's health was also improving. "He's keeping himself clean and spending time with us," she expressed with gratitude. When my cousin was on the spiral downward, he would stop washing himself for weeks on end and roam the streets. At the end of our call, I remember being so grateful and happy that tragedy had been avoided.

Leading up to that moment, memorial services were a large reason that I visited LA so consistently. So, I was thankful to not have to make another trip out there so soon.

That was until three months later, when I got a frantic call from my father. Auntie was in the hospital in critical condition. "What?!" I exclaimed. "She had been fine just a couple months ago!" I assumed that something had happened with her kidney, but nothing could have prepared me for the story I was to receive. For those faint of heart, please read this with caution.

My cousin's mental health had regressed. He stopped bathing and was back to roaming the streets. One day, when he had returned home, my aunt asked him to shower and to keep himself clean. This triggered my cousin, and soon a fight broke out. In a fit of rage, my dear cousin knocked my aunt, his mother, on the ground and fatally wounded her, fleeing the house shortly after.

Her stepson heard the commotion from downstairs and frantically ran up the stairs to see her bleeding profusely on the floor. He called 911, and when they arrived, she was rushed to the hospital, where she remained in intensive care.

When I heard the news, I immediately went into a deep meditation. I connected with my aunt's spirit, begging her to stay, and sent her positive energy through the ethereal realm. I felt her presence as a bright golden light, a confirmation that she would stay long enough for me to say goodbye. I also felt that while she was no longer in pain, she was spiritually tired, ready to return home. This made her eventual passing, after we arrived at the hospital, a bit easier.

While I couldn't speak with her in the physical realm, I was able to say goodbye to her in the spiritual realm. And to those reading this story who have lost dear ones, I send you infinite unconditional love and compassion for your losses. The silver lining is that through activating your V.I.S.A. and leveling up your 6Cs, you will have tools to connect with those who have passed to the other side. The key is Compassion. The key is connecting to your heart.

It is through this connection that I have felt the presence of my aunt in my life ever since. My brother, sister, uncles, and grandparents as well.

There was a detail I left out from the last visit I had with my aunt back in 2015. She had made me promise that no matter what happened to her, I would look after her son. At the time, I didn't want to think that my aunt wouldn't be around, but after her passing, I accepted that I needed to honor this promise and to not let her sacrifice be in vain. My cousin now could get the medical attention he needed, as long as he didn't end up being convicted. He needed our collective support to inspire the judge to grant him innocence by plea of "insanity," and support him we did. Through tears of sadness, our family rallied around him so that he could receive the treatment he desperately needed in a mental facility. I remember when that verdict was announced, my heart was sore, but also grateful that he would have a chance of being the jovial, carefree young man I remembered him as.

A couple of years later, once he was in a stable location, I reached out to him. When he picked up the phone with a curious, "Hello?" It was the first time in years that I heard my cousin's authentic voice. I cried tears of joy as I walked through a park in Brooklyn. We talked about his workouts, his progress of healing his childhood traumas, and his prospects of getting into a halfway house in the upcoming years if he kept improving. I gave him a breathwork exercise to do as well, and we've stayed in contact ever since. He's healing, and it was the unconditional love of his mother, who offered her life in order for her child to be okay, that made it possible.

This is the power of love in action, this is the power of unconditional love, this is the power of compassion. And because this is the emotion connected with the heart chakra, the energy center of our heart, where our first brain exists, it's imperative for us to lean into this space to also transform our own lives. This next quest is going to simplify the process by tapping into our imagination to create a safe space, to explore the vulnerability of the heart.

Imagine you are a highly advanced spaceship, like the *SS Enterprise* or *Millenium Falcon*, navigating through the vast expanse of the universe. In this analogy, the brain serves as your navigation system, providing critical guidance, strategies, and calculations to chart your course. Your heart, however, is the coveted "warp drive" to your spaceship. It is the powerful engine that allows you to travel to your desired destination faster than the speed of light, transcending light and logic.

In life, your brain serves as the tool you use to set your goals, the destinations you desire to reach in the future. It's essential for charting the challenges you might face along the way and prepares you for the journey by reminding you of the skills you'll need to develop to get there. What drives you to fulfill these requirements to reach your goals is the energy of the heart. Your heart fuels your journey with passion, gratitude, and compassion, love in action. It's the driving force that enables you to clear the obstacles that hold the XP needed to level up your life.

But what if we've been so caught up with the destination and the obstacles, that we've forgotten to listen to the heart? Our own warp drive can't deliver us to our dreams because it's being slowed down by fear of obstacles that are only meant to remind us of our gifts.

This is why, in the upcoming guided journey, we are going to hit the ESC button and drop into our Imagination Realization Realm to journey into a sacred space within our hearts, to observe and reactivate it to serve our highest possible good.

This is one of my favorite journeys, and it's going to unlock a special place within your IRR that is quintessentially YOU.

MISSION 15A: SACRED HEART JOURNEY - OBSERVATION

This next experience is going to change the way you live life, even more than the previous ones. We've used our imagination to construct objects and screens to support our journey, but we haven't used it to create our very own world. Today we are going to start small and start with us. I'll see you in the LTUVG app.

Mission 15a Activated
Open the LTUVG App and access Mission 15a:
Sacred Heart Sanctuary Journey: Observation

How do you feel? What did you see? Do you remember what your portal looks like? When you found your sacred space did it feel like home at first? Was it easy or hard to accept that this was your sacred space? Journal your feelings and then sketch what your sacred heart sanctuary looked like. It's important to write down/draw everything you experienced in the journey, because it will help you access it the next time you do this journey.

MISSION 15B: RENOVATING YOUR SACRED HEART SANCTUARY!

The next part of this mission involves journeying back into your Sacred Heart Sanctuary for some "renovating" or "upgrading."

As a general rule, please wait a day before trying this. Or, if you have the time and energy, let's prepare to journey back into your SHS. Make sure that you complete the previous mission and upload a sketch of your Sacred Heart Sanctuary to the app.

Your mission, should you choose to accept it, is to readjust your sacred space to match what you feel it should look like today. If you want more nature in it, bring more trees into the space, add animals; if it's too busy, take the busy-ness out and make it quieter. There are no limitations to this. Jump into the LTUVG app, enjoy, and have fun!

Mission 15b Activated
Open the LTUVG App and access Mission 15b:
Renovating Your Sacred Heart Sanctuary

And just like that we have unlocked another skill tree for Compassion! You can also now take this awareness and access old practices, such as the Tonglen meditation, to see how much easier you can send and receive love from your heart. The more that you can get your heart to feel like the sun, the more energy you will be putting out into your YOUniverse to support your goals and connect with those whom you've lost along your own journey.

With practice you will use the 3,2,1 method with breathwork to drop into this space like Zai and me. It will be your tool to quickly tap into warp drive. Consistently practice and it will help you travel faster than the speed of light to your goals!

Level 7 Recap:

- Subtle Energy XP/Grinding Activities
    - Sacred Heart Sanctuary Journey/Renovations

LEVEL 8

REACTIVATING YOUR CREATIVITY

QUEST 16 - IMAGINATION ACTIVATION

Before we go further, I wanted to say thank you for your dedication to yourself! It takes courage to step into the unknown and trust the voice in your heart that may be contradictory to what society has made you believe. A society that has tried to convince us that our imagination isn't real, that we must be practical to find success in life, and that happiness must be pursued. These were the limiting beliefs that I was taught growing up. This is why I fell in love with video games, to explore worlds created by someone's imagination. It was the manifestation of the imagination into a realm that I could play in. It was an escape from my own painful reality.

The pursuit of happiness creates the illusion that happiness is outside of us, When it was within, all along.

I wish I had known this truth as a kid. But my upbringing was laced with too much pain. I got used to losing things at an incredibly early age. My sister Diana passed away when I was three years old. I lost the safety of my home in my parents' divorce before I was a teenager. And as my father was struggling to make ends meet, I lost the surety of what I might eat daily. Then, when I was in college, my grandfather passed away. A month later we lost our younger brother Tristen, and to cap it all off, I nearly died in a motorcycle accident that took two years to heal from. This doesn't include the tragic deaths of my aunt, uncles, grandparents, and cousins.

Amid this loss, just like a good video game, I became the hero. I was determined to go to college, get a well-paying job, and build a safety net for my family so they never had to stress about money again. So that they could have space to heal from the tragic loss in our family.

How did I process these losses? I got good, masterful even, at compartmentalizing pain. But my outlet was always video games. Big adventures where, despite many tragic events, the hero accomplished a mission and "saved" somebody or sometimes, the world. *Final Fantasy* games were my favorite, and I put hundreds of hours into these games to make sure that I unlocked any and everything. One of the things that pulled me deeply into the game was the immense imagination that these games exhibited.

Take a moment, close your eyes, and visualize the game that you appreciated the most for its imagination. Maybe even do a quick HMC technique so that you can enter the alpha state of consciousness to make this world even that much more illustrious.

10, 9, 8, 7, 6, 5, 4, 3, 2, 1... You are now visualizing your favorite game on your movie screen. Observe and when you are ready, come back here.

How did that feel? Where did you go? Did your heart feel warm, and were you filled with good memories of when you played and completed that game? Was it a bittersweet experience instead? Log it if you feel like it. Good, we are going to use this energy to help level up the vividness of your Imagination Realization Station.

To help illustrate the scientific basis for the imagination pulling information from a place of inner knowing, let's explore some intriguing research done on Alzheimer's patients that reveals the connections between memory and imagination.

Alzheimer's is a degenerative disease where people slowly lose their short-term memory and eventually long-term memory. It's a difficult disease to experience because your loved ones eventually forget who you are to them. It's a sickness that both Zai'Ra and I experienced with our grandfathers before they transitioned. Interestingly, a study published in the *Journal of Cognitive Neuroscience* found that Alzheimer's patients show parallel deficits in recalling past events and imagining future ones.[61] The same brain region, namely the hippocampus, is active in both memory retrieval and future event simulation.

These findings provide compelling evidence that our imagination is not just a fanciful exercise but is rooted in the same cognitive framework that governs our memories. When we imagine the future, we are drawing from the same well of inner knowledge that holds our past experiences. This interconnectedness supports the concept that creativity and intuitive insights are based on a deep-seated cognitive foundation.

The origins of the word "imagination" even supports this concept. Imagination comes from the Greek root's *imago*, meaning "likeness of something," and *natio*, which refers to a collective or group of related things. Our imagination, therefore, is a projection of images that are made up of us, also know, as our soul. What ancient teachers refer to as the manifestation of our soul's inner knowing.

To help make this concept more relatable, let's tap into another gaming analogy, imagining our mind as an expansive, open-world video game. Something akin to *Zelda: Breath of the Wild*, *Skyrim*, or *Final Fantasy*. In these games, as you explore the landscapes you are given quests that you need to complete to move the story forward, unlocking areas of the map as well, that are logged into your saved data. Think of your memory

---

[61] Addis, D. R., et al. (2012). Linking the past to the future: Memory and imagination in the brain. *Journal of Cognitive Neuroscience.*

as the progress that you make throughout the game, and your imagination as a continuation of the missions you've already completed. Your inner knowing is a projection of this information communicated to you, the main character, through NPCs, non-player characters. Like people living with Alzheimer's, if you don't have access to the information gained from exploring the map and completing each quest, then the NPCs cannot communicate with your imagination what the next quest might be.

So, as we are building up our Imagination Realization Realm, let's think of our imagination as an extension of the NPCs in our mind providing us with information to finish the quests we are completing in this instruction manual. This quote from Bob Proctor might help solidify this concept further:

"If you can picture it in your mind, you can hold it in your hand."

And today's activity starts with picturing fruit and, if you want to activate a bonus mission, bring a piece of fruit in your home for a special bonus ability.

MISSION 16: FRUIT LOOPER

Before we sit with another guided journey, I want to make sure that your inner voice is supporting your journey. What is your inner voice? Well, even as you are reading this book, there is a voice repeating the words that you are reading in your head. Stop reading, and see if the voice stops; now start reading again, is it back? Crazy, right? If you never noticed this before, be more aware of when this voice is present and how it's communicating with you.

Refer to the Self-Love Quests' if there is still negative self-talk that you are hearing, especially in this exercise. This is because "doubt" has the power to deflate any visualizations our imagination is creating. It's okay that the doubt is there, it's just old programming designed to keep you stuck in limiting beliefs. Noticing it means that you are starting to wake up. If that is the case, write this down somewhere where you can read it often:

My imagination empowers my
ability to activate my dreams,
My imagination improves every time I use it.

Alright, we're ready. Let's get our LTUVG app out and explore our subconscious in Mission 16.

Mission 16 Activated
Open the LTUVG App and access Mission 16:
Fruit Looper

Amazing job! Give yourself a lot of encouragement because this is not necessarily an easy exercise.

Now, if you have your fruit with you in your "gaming sanctuary," bring it out and lets jump into this bonus mission in the LTUVG app.

Bonus Mission 16 Activated

Open the LTUVG App and access Bonus Mission 16: *Fruit Whisperer*

Wow! Nice Life Gamer, you are crushing the visualization and projection game. Give yourself some grace and we'll take a break for the day, but for tomorrow you'll need to do two things. Find two plants, ask permission to take one leaf from each, and bring them for tomorrow's quest. Just make sure that each plant is of different textures. One firm, the other soft, for example.

QUEST 17 - GREENTHUMB STATE OF MIND

Are you having fun yet? Remembering when you were a kid playing with curiosity? If there is still some resistance, that's perfectly normal, it will click soon. If you are having trouble with the changing color part of the exercise, please spend another day with the activity. There is no rush to this inspirational manual, please progress at your own pace. Let go of control, of feeling like you "don't know what you're doing," and pretend you are playing a new video game that's teaching you as you go. That is what we are effectively doing. We are learning how to replay a game that we forgot had magic in it. To relearn how to play life by awakening these gifts can feel like learning a new game mode in a game you've mastered already.

Imagine your favorite game just released a new game mode where you have to learn an entirely new combat system. It's going to seem complex at first, and you might be tempted to play through the game's world leaning on your old skillset, but the new skills and strategies are the only abilities that will level up the game's new skill trees. You are still adapting to this new game mode, but as you shift your perspective on this paradigm shift, your IR Station will feel more natural as well as the mental screen.

For those who are getting a handle on their Imagination Realization Station mental screens, let's try the next quest and take our first stab at remote viewing! This time, we are going to do a visualization and connection with the physical presence of two different types of plants.

Do you have two leaves? Did you ask permission? If you thought I was joking, I wasn't. This is based on my own experiences with plant consciousness, and "decades of experiments, [where] plants are starting to be regarded as beings capable of calculation and choice, learning and memory."[62] Stefano Mancuso, leading plant neurobiologist, gives some interesting TED talks on plant consciousness and the growing recognition of plants as intelligent beings capable of complex behaviors. When we engage with taking from plants, asking permission just keeps us from developing negative XP when it could otherwise avoid it.

Okay, with your two leaves in hand, let's jump into the LTUVG app and level up our imagination realization realm!

---

[62] Mancuso, S. (2015). *Brilliant Green: The Surprising History and Science of Plant Intelligence*. Island Press.

MISSION 17: PLANT WHISPERER

Mission 17 Activated
Open the LTUVG App and access Mission 17:
Plant Whisperer

How are you feeling? A bit like your mind and emotions are going in different directions? You are making energetic connections with living things on earth in a new way while your brain is trying to reconcile these new experiences with what "modern science" has told you. That's okay. Remember we are suspending our disbelief, so that the experiences speak for themselves. There is nothing wrong with feeling more, in fact, that's how we are going to expand our abilities at a precipitous rate.

You've already spent much of your life using the skills you are used to. Our goal now is to massively improve your V.I.S.A., which we can level up exponentially by focusing on leveling up our 6Cs skill trees. Feelings and premonitions you have will continue to roll into "coincidences" that only you can explain. Let these be the little breadcrumbs that you are on the right path.

Like the white rabbit from *The Matrix*, this is your game, and life will give you the hints that you are ready to receive. That's what this chapter has focused on, increasing your creativity so that you can be more open to play in the day. With more play, you will start to see the synchronicities guiding you on your intended path.

Your brain is like an open-world game,
Using past experiences to unlock new
quests and future adventures.
Harness your imagination to explore new
possibilities and create your reality.

With that we've completed half of the Universal 6C Principles. Let's just do a quick overview of them and how they support each other and your V.I.S.A. Attributes.

- **Consistency:**
  - Purpose: Consistency is the foundation that allows you to practice the skills necessary to level up in the game of life. By being consistent, you build habits and routines that strengthen your abilities and resilience.
  - Connection to Compassion: On days when consistency falters, compassion steps in. It provides the grace to forgive yourself, preventing the demotivation that can come from missed steps.
- **Compassion:**
  - Purpose: Compassion supports you during the times when consistency is hard to maintain. It gives you a safe haven, a camp to rest at, and introduces your first imaginary construct—the sacred heart sanctuary—that you can portal into for emotional and mental rejuvenation.
  - Connection to Creativity: Similar to our root and sacral chakras, once you have established a safe space through

compassion, you have the freedom to explore and tap into your creativity. The secure foundation of compassion allows your mind to wander and experiment without fear of judgment or failure.

- **Creativity:**
  - Purpose: Creativity is the core of the Imagination Realization Station, enabling you to visualize new solutions, dream up new possibilities, and innovate in your personal and professional life. Creativity flows naturally from compassion because a compassionate environment nurtures creative thinking by reducing stress and opening the mind to new ideas.

What is the next Universal Principle that Creativity connects to? Well now that our imagination is engaged and activated, generating ideas and possibilities freely, we need a filtration system. This is where CLARITY becomes essential to sift through the thousands of ideas we're producing. Allowing us to focus on what truly matters and make clear decisions that creatively guide us to our goals.

Level 8 Recap:

- Subtle Energy XP/Grinding Activities
  - Fruit Looper
  - Plant Whisperer

LEVEL 9

CREATING CLARITY

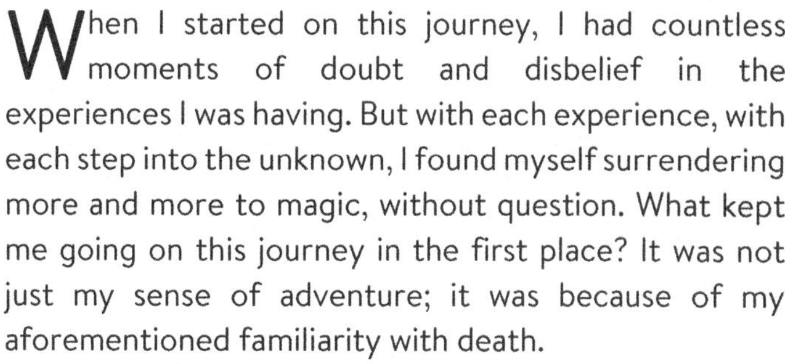

When I started on this journey, I had countless moments of doubt and disbelief in the experiences I was having. But with each experience, with each step into the unknown, I found myself surrendering more and more to magic, without question. What kept me going on this journey in the first place? It was not just my sense of adventure; it was because of my aforementioned familiarity with death.

By the time I had my own near-death experience, it no longer frightened me. The experience of loss in my life drove me to find a way to heal the wounds that these tragedies created. Along the way, I discovered someone else who had a near death experience, but who wasn't as lucky as I was to walk away from it, at least not right away.

Dr. Joe Dispenza was, for a time, a chiropractor living his normal life out in California. One day, as he was riding his bicycle home, a Ford Bronco hit him from behind. Joe woke up in the hospital, unable to move his legs, paralyzed from the waist down. Joe was "lucky" to be alive, with seven broken vertebrae in his back.

When the doctors gave Joe the prognosis and a bleak outlook on his prospects of walking again, he didn't accept those terms. In his mind, he thought, ""[If] I focus on creating a clear intention of what I want... [with an] elevated mood, I [can] signal new genes in new ways." With this optimistic attitude and determination, Joe was eventually walking again, defying medical expectations.[63]

How was he able to consistently create healing in his body? He had clarity of what he wanted to accomplish with a clear elevated emotion. That is why our fourth Universal Principle used to tap into our subtle realm powers is Clarity.

Decades after his miraculous healing, Dr. Dispenza has written multiple books, one of which, *Becoming Supernatural*, was an encyclopedia for me for over a year. Convinced that common people can also accomplish the "impossible," he has gone on to teach tens of thousands of people to enter elevated states of consciousness to miraculously heal themselves of cancer, autoimmune diseases, chronic psychosomatic illnesses, and more.[64]

---

[63] Dispenza, J. (2014). *You Are the Placebo: Making Your Mind Matter*. Hay House, Inc.

[64] Dispenza, J. (2017). Becoming Supernatural: How Common People Are Doing the Uncommon. Hay House, Inc.

Dr. Dispenza also has the data to support "how" it happens.[65] His guidance and ability to "demystify" things such as meditation and quantum medicine inspired me to write this book! To demystify the fabric of the Universe and how it works by connecting it with the world of video games! To break down the complexity of how clarity can show up in our lives, we are going to break them into three parts: clarity of mind, clarity in purpose, and clarity of heart.

QUEST 18 - CLARITY OF MIND

First, let's talk about Clarity of Mind. Remember that our conscious mind is only able to process 30-40 bits of information per second? In contrast, our subconscious mind processes eleven million bits of information per second! A bit is a basic unit of information used to quantify the amount of information the brain can manage at any given moment. But for a rough comparison, this would be like comparing the computing power of a 1990 Mac Computer to 100+ 2024 MacBook Pros, relatively.

So how do we survive if our conscious mind is only processing a fraction of what our subconscious mind is absorbing? We have a network of neurons in the brainstem called the Reticular Activating System (RAS) which filters the massive amount of info received from

---

[65] T. Leys, Heather Khoo, S. Lee (2020). Large effects of brief meditation intervention on EEG spectra in meditation novices. Consciousness and Cognition, 83, 82020. https://doi.org/10.1016/j.concog.2020.102974

our senses, bringing relevant data to our conscious awareness to regulate our arousal state.[66]

To understand this a little more clearly, let's continue to build off our open-world gaming analogy for the brain from the previous chapter. In any open-world game, there are thousands, if not millions of pieces of information that are being calculated. For instance, the enemies spawning, the weather, the time of day, NPCs, and all of the interactions your character is making with the world have lines of code stored in the database of the game. But for the controller of the game, they just have their heads-up display showing them the relevant information to their game.

Remember, accessing our HUD allows us to get a conscious window into our subconscious mind. But just like the conscious mind, the HUD in a game only shows us critical information like health, stamina, mission objectives and a minimap. It doesn't display data that isn't crucial to the main character's missions.

Following this analogy, our RAS is effectively our Quest Log Manager. In any game, you have a quest log that tracks all of your current missions, but you typically have the ability to select a few of them that will be displayed on your HUD. It would be great if we had control over which mission objectives were displayed in our HUD, but this is only possible if we engage in metacognition to observe how our RAS is choosing the missions to be displayed.

---

[66] García-Rill, E. (2015). Waking and the Reticular Activating System in Health and Disease. Academic Press.

For example, if you are living with anxiety about public speaking, your RAS is going to bring things to your attention based on these concerns. You might become hyper-aware of opportunities to speak in public, but instead of seeing them as chances for growth, your RAS flags them as potential threats to avoid.

Our RAS doesn't discriminate between 'good' or 'bad' scenarios; it simply highlights what it perceives as most important for our survival based on our past experiences and current focus. In this case, as we move through life encountering various 'NPCs' (people) who could potentially offer opportunities for personal or professional growth, our internal HUD might be flashing warning signs. Instead of seeing a networking event as a chance to make valuable connections, your RAS might label it as a dangerous situation to be avoided at all costs.

This selective attention works both ways. Just as someone with social anxiety might be overly attuned to potential social threats, someone with a more positive outlook might be more likely to notice and remember friendly faces in a crowd or opportunities for positive interactions. It's similar to how two people can experience the same situation but come away with completely different perspectives – one seeing challenges and risks, the other seeing opportunities and potential rewards.

If your RAS sends your HUD information which isn't taking you to new goals you have set, how do you recalibrate it? You would use metacognition. We've mentioned this concept before, but we'll now go through another exercise to work on reprogramming your mind with a bit more awareness and energy.

Think of metacognition as unlocking your ability to observe which missions are being filtered to your HUD and choose which quest will appear in the HUD moving forward. This will allow you to reframe negative or fear-based thoughts and consciously choose to focus on positive, growth-oriented goals without the negative subconscious thoughts undermining you.

We are trying to do that with all of our subconscious memories. We want to become aware of our subconscious mind, the thoughts swirling in there, so that we can clean up the ones that no longer serve us. The subconscious thoughts that tell us that "we can't accomplish that", that "we are afraid of failing", that "we always ____"—insert said limiting belief.

Similar to cognitive therapy, this book trains you to expand your beliefs, so that you can fly to your destiny.[67] A destiny that your higher self has been pulling you toward all of your life.

MISSION 18A: INTUITION'S CONTROLLER

This is one of my favorite meditations! It's a way to engage with all of your thoughts, new and old, and decide which ones still serve your highest vibrational path, and which ones can be let go with gratitude!

---

[67] Beck, A. T. (1991). Cognitive therapy: A 30-year retrospective. American psychologist, 46(4), 368.

But first, you have to gain one of my favorite multidimensional constructs to quiet the mind on your own!

Remember when we mentioned that the analytical mind and intuition inversely affect one another? Such that when the analytical mind is super active, our intuition is not able to communicate with us through our inner knowing.

To prepare you for today's meditation and give you a tool to instantly quiet the analytical mind, you are going to visualize a knob, a controller to turn down the thoughts coming from your analytical mind. And it's going to be AWESOME.

So, let's jump into the LTUVG app for this quick tool that will help to expand the connection with your inner knowing.

Mission 18a Activated
Open the LTUVG App and access Mission 18a:
Intuition's Controller

Great work master builder! Now you have the power to not just use this imaginary construct, but the ability to create other knobs to control your anxiety, fear, energy, and more! With imagination as your greatest gifts, your only limitation is your expectation.

MISSION 18B: SPRING CLEANING THE MIND

Let's employ this new skill to spring clean your mind to make room for all the amazing gifts coming online. See you in the LTUVG app!

Mission 18b Activated
Open the LTUVG App and access Mission 18b:
Spring Cleaning Journey

Amazing, you now have two tools that you can use to actively create clarity of mind in your life. Not only will you minimize the number of thoughts distracting and draining you of energy on your quest to rescue your inner child, but you will also create space for new thoughts to come in that will guide you to your dreams! But what are those dreams?

When you are aligned with your destiny, the Universe will usher you there with a quickness, but first, you must have clarity of what that is. Tomorrow, we'll use an essential tool to clear the pathway to our purpose.

Until then, have fun with your new analytical mind remote controller.

QUEST 19 - CLARITY OF PURPOSE

Have you ever been curious why it's easier for you to wake up for things that you are passionate about as opposed to those things that you don't want to do? Like the night before Christmas, when my parents were still together, my brother and I couldn't wait to get up and race down the stairs to see what presents we were given.

At that time, I wasn't aware of how lucky and blessed we were to have a home with two parents, a dog, and a pool. My parents weren't rich, but they put all of their love into their family. It took years for me to understand why. I mentioned before that I had a sister who passed away at a very young age. Here's how it helped provide a clear purpose not just for my parents, but for my siblings and me as well.

My parents were ecstatic when Diana was born. She was the third and final child my mom and dad had planned on having, and they had both prayed for a daughter. I remember seeing a video during her only winter with my mom and dad taking care of her, and it was clear that she had something that she was fighting to survive. It turned out to be a weak heart, and she succumbed to this disease shortly after. It broke my parents' hearts, and they struggled to put the pieces back together.

With an immense amount of courage, my mom and dad tried to have another child. When Victoria, my second sister, was born, she brought immediate healing to us all. It wasn't until she got married that we collectively realized how.

My brothers and sisters are a big reason why I have been determined to continue on my healing journey. Sometimes referred to as the "super siblings," the bond between my brothers and sisters is impenetrable. And it was all from the sacrifice of my eldest sister, Diana.

It was her loss that reminded us of the value of life, to make the most of the gifts we have. As a result, while my mom and dad were the first in their family to attend college, our determination to persevere through difficult times produced 3 ivy league graduates. My sister even got a double masters from Berkeley after graduating from Stanford, smarty pants.

This **clarity in purpose** that gives people a strong direction in life is the same purpose that brought me here, to write this book. The words on these pages are dedicated first and foremost to my brave parents, inspirational brothers and sisters, in this realm and the next, and to Zai'Ra, the love of lifetimes.

Take the adventure of Zelda. Every time, without fail, princess Zelda gets captured by Ganondorf and locked in a castle somewhere. And every time, without fail, Link is tasked with leveling up and gaining the weapons necessary to defeat Ganondorf. At the beginning of any epic adventure, our purpose must be clear. It's the magnet that pulls us through the tough times and keeps us grounded in gratitude because we know what true loss feels like. The hero perseveres through the obstacles before them because they know the pain of loss, and they'll do whatever it takes to keep that loss from happening again. Link never hesitates, and when you have your clarity of purpose, you will find motivation to keep leveling up your life in the same manner.

Remember your first purpose in this book—to rescue your inner child from the prison of life's traumas that has separated you from them. With every practice of breathwork, meditation, visualization, or bio-hack, you are one step closer to that fateful day. Every soul shard or GOU earned along the way brings you one quest closer to your inner you.

MISSION 19: THE 4 MOST IMPORTANT QUESTIONS (4MIQS)

You know you're on a journey to rescue your inner child, but what happens after that? What will rescuing your inner child grant you access to? This next exercise is going to provide a road map, quite literally, of the experiences in life you can attain as you work your way to rescuing your inner child. You are going to create this road map yourself by answering these four very important questions.

1. The Experiences you want to have in life.
2. How you will Grow to achieve these experiences.
3. How you will Contribute to the world around you in exchange.
4. How you will Feel when you are living those experiences.

This is one of my favorite missions! See you in the LTUVG app!

Mission 19 Activated
Open the LTUVG App and access Mission 19:
The 4 Most Important Questions

How do you feel? Empowered now that you have a list of goals you will experience and accomplish in your life? If you have butterflies in your stomach or nervous energy, that's a good sign! It means you are dreaming big.

If you haven't shared your list of goals with the community yet, take a photo or screenshot of each list, and share it in the "4MIQ Bulletin Board" Channel in the LGG community. This is a sure-fire way to reach these goals faster and earn an easy contribution experience point.

This is because offering your answers to the community will inspire others, who may even adapt them for themselves. And that's okay! There isn't a monopoly on dreams.

In addition, just like gaining XP for your clan, this will connect your 4MIQs to everyone else's answers. As you check something off your list, it contributes to the community's growth, which benefits everyone.

QUEST 20 - CLARITY OF HEART

Do you remember the movie Braveheart?

There is an iconic scene where the main character, William Wallace, is leading the Scottish into battle. They are facing a British army that has them outnumbered, and he has to convince the Scots to go into battle. The Scots were fighting for their freedom, sovereignty over their ability to live, breathe, and decide their own future. They now stood at the precipice of a deciding battle. Either they would be victorious, and the British armies would retreat, or they would fail and die, shattering any chances of freedom. Wallace gave a speech that enraptured his men, culminating in the line:

> ***"They can take our lives, but they can never take our FREEDOM!"***

How powerful is that? That you can convince thousands of men that their lives are eternal. No matter if they lose their physical bodies, they will die with their freedom intact. This is what Clarity of Heart can create for the human spirit. If you haven't seen the movie, I won't ruin the ending.

What if we were able to approach each day with this same faith in our purpose? We'd first need to find that purpose, but what if there was a hack to let life guide us there?

What are your passions? Let's utilize our answers from the 4MIQ to remember what inspired our inner heart to come to earth.

MISSION 20: SEED MEDITATION

To help create clarity on your heart's purpose(s) in this lifetime, you must return to the womb, to when you were just a seed in your mother's belly. Today's journey is going to help with this, and there is a high chance that a GOU is earned from this if you surrender completely to the guided journey. If you're ready to level up, let's jump in together for a healing ancestral ride.

Mission 20 Activated
Open the LTUVG App and access Mission 20:
Seed Meditation

How did it feel to return to being a seed? Or to get a sense of what it was like to be inside of a star, waiting to come to earth? Pretty magical huh? If you are still in limbo somewhere between being a seed in Mother Earth and in the cosmos, keep journaling, keep trusting what your heart is showing you. Remember to ground yourself if you still are floating after that.

The magic you are feeling is real, the memories you are accessing are real. How it's connecting with your childhood and possibly forgotten memories are clearing a pathway back to yourself, back to your inner child.

These are all check marks helping to level you up to rescue your inner child. Each memory, a breadcrumb, reminding you a bit more of where your inner child is hiding. Take your time with each memory. Journal, laugh, cry, connect with your family as questions come up, and keep forgiving and giving unconditional love to yourself and others to support this adventure. You are exactly where you are supposed to be.

Once you have done this exercise for seven days, you will be ready to enter your second "Boss Quest."

During these seven days, feel free to update your 4MIQ list for yourself. We do this journey for seven days because each time you connect more and more with your soul spark, the spark that brought you to Mother

Earth. Eventually, a GOU or two will come to you that will help with the upcoming Boss Quest.

SAVE POINT 4: APPROACHING THE SUMMIT

And with that, we've reached our fourth save point to review how far you've come thus far.

With your seven-day quest with the Seed Meditation, this is a perfect time to take a week or so and deepen your practice with this mission, and any others that you feel called to enjoy. Trust your intuition and current life situation to guide your daily missions.

If you have any complications or blockages with the Seed Meditation, feel free to send me a message via the app and I will reach back out. But first, try doing the Spring Cleaning Journey.

After you complete the Seed Meditation journey, remember to complete the mission log AND submit your experiences to the "Real Life WINS" channel in the Life Gamer Guild and celebrate!

Finally, jump into the Save Point 4 Mission in the LTUVG app to receive your new Skill Codex and your new skill assessments! You now have Compassion, Creativity, and Clarity to upgrade. Let's gooooo.

And once these are complete, you'll be ready to activate your full energetic self.

! Save Point 4: !

Approaching the Summit Unlocked

Go to LTUVG App

BOSS QUEST 2 - BLESSING OF THE CHAKRAS

If you are here, that means that you've completed the seven-day quest to reconnect with your soul's spark. Congratulations! How does it feel?

Do you feel inspired to step into your purpose and start to bring your spirit avatar, your eternal monk, or dragon lancer through the subtle energy realm and into the physical? To open this portal, you must journey inward and be completely vulnerable. And in this space of surrender, ask for guidance and connect with a visualization of your inner knowing. The lower realm is what shamans refer to as our intuitive connection with our inner knowing. It's our Imagination Realization Realm (IRR).

I've been teaching you how to create this realm for yourself throughout this inspiration manual. Eventually, we are going to imagine meeting our sacred spirit animal (SSA) there, with an open mind. A brief history of spirit animals, they are animals of this earth, and sometimes mythical, that take form in the subtle energy realm. They are an extension of you; these companions are like companions in RPGs that give you physical, spiritual, and emotional support as you navigate life.

Before I teach you, you must complete the upcoming boss mission. But the reward will be well worth the effort of this 45-minute guided meditation. To prepare you, let me share an epic story of my own IRR.

The first time I journeyed to my lower realm it was a fantastical environment. Like out of *Final Fantasy* or

Elder Scrolls. There were fields of grass that stretched to the ocean, with a forest of lush trees that protected my SHS as well as an ancient pyramid. But standing out like Mordor, was a tall, dark mountain covered in clouds, which I called Shadow Mountain.

Up until Zai'Ra and I first met, I had avoided this mountain and the demons (or skeletons) that resided there. Zai gave me the courage to finally face my demons that I had been running from for most of my life. And the very first time that I ventured up Shadow Mountain, I had to vanquish a vampire.

To be clear, this is NOT a version of a spirit animal. But my spirit animal did help me complete this mission. You see, this vampire wasn't just a regular run of the mill vamp. It knew all of my weaknesses and the things it could tempt me with. He was creating havoc in my life by harming everyone I cared about. I snuck into his lair, but when I peeked into his casket, I was shocked to see that the vampire looked just like me! Wait... was I the person responsible for this?

I couldn't handle this raw truth. I turned to run away, but as I approached the door I was ripped from behind and thrown on the floor with the bloodsucker on top of me (dramatic I know). It was at this moment that I called on Arthur, my power animal, to help. Arthur was an amazing monkey who never let me down, either with his intelligence or humor.

He wisely handed me a stake that I plunged into my doppelganger vampire. As the vampire disintegrated into a blood red amulet, I felt like I freed a part of myself from guilt and shame. But that mission wasn't over. I had to take the amulet back to my Sacred Heart Sanctuary and purify it in a pool. Once I did, my weakness to the temptations of strip clubs, porn, and more, were gone.

Ever since that moment, I continued to make regular visits to this mountain, clearing levels to release the negative energy that still resided within me. In the spiritual realm, we call this "shadow work," and it is a sacred practice of recovering our own light, GOUs, soul shards and even soul fragments from the darkest places within us. Soul fragments are just bigger versions of soul shards. I would say that I recovered a full soul fragment from this next mission.

By the time we were in ceremony with Kanna, I had cleared most of the levels on this mountain. But in order to see myself as I was, I had to heal the entire mountain. One of the final levels on this mountain was atop the mountain, in an arena with my grandfather.

If you remember, this was the same ceremony where Zaï'Ra was bursting with celestial light while I spiraled into darkness. While I was in this dark place, I had asked to be taken to a safe place, which dropped me into my lower realm. But I wasn't in my normal SHS, instead I was standing at the foot of Shadow Mountain. Taken aback and a little scared, I called on Arthur.

"What is going on?" I asked, which is the typical question you should ask your guides in confusing moments.

Arthur looked at me as if to say, "The same thing we do every time we are here, we go up."

I knew this was what he would say, and although I was more nervous than I had been the last time I ventured up the mountain, I felt a nurturing presence with me as well. "You are safe," I heard from the whisper of the presence of Kanna, as I started to make my way up the long winding pathway.

Continuing up the rocky mountain, I had a flashback of my last moment with my Uncle Michael, who had transitioned a couple years back. He was a nurse who had diabetes and essentially ate himself to his own demise with sugar. He was such a bright soul before this but suffered from being the smallest of the four boys in my grandfather's household. He didn't get the love and praise that my dad and his other brothers got for their athleticism and strength. As my uncle's life began to decline, he couldn't work anymore, and shortly thereafter, lost his home. He moved in with his son Jason, who I would also see in LA on my visits.

It was November of 2018 when I saw my Uncle Michael for the last time. When I arrived in LA Jason asked if I would go visit his father, who was now at a homeless shelter. Taken aback that he was no longer at Jason's house, I soon learned that Jason, too, was without shelter. He was living out of his car and couldn't take care of his father, who had just had a stroke, but there was more to the story. What I learned next was heartbreaking. Uncle Michael, after this stroke, had become incontinent, had lost his will to live, and was not on good terms with either of his kids.

From listening, I knew that my uncle could use some unconditional love, a big hug, and some depends, adult diapers. As I arrived at the shelter and got through their security with his resources, the gravity of his situation began to sink in. We take much in life for granted, and it hit me like a ton of bricks when I saw this warehouse of cots stacked on one another like out of a war film. There were hundreds of men there, who had nothing but the clothes on their backs; there was a strong stench of body odor and an energy of stagnation in the air. It felt like a forgotten place where souls are in a holding cell waiting for something.

As I walked up to my uncle's cot, I was filled with joy when I saw him. I didn't care what his state was, just seeing him alive brought warmth to my heart. Honoring the intimate details of this moment, I will share that his condition reverted him back to being an infant in a grown man's body. Without a caretaker, living a stable life was nearly impossible. For that afternoon, I had the honor of being his caretaker and got him freshened-up in new clothes and undergarments.

There was something surreal and sacred about holding my uncle as if he was a child in a life-worn body. It gave me context to how special life on earth is and how much we lose as we transition out of this realm. As our time came to a close, his spirits were lifted, and I left him with some cash to enjoy some of the sweeter things in life in his last moments with us.

As the last memory with my uncle faded into the ether, I approached the top of the mountain. Much like climbing the throat of the world in *Skyrim*, there was an ominous presence as I stood at the archway atop the mountain, which opened into a clearing of dirt in the shape of a circle with ridges of rocks all around it. Walking into the arena, I felt a presence to my right. To my surprise, it was my Uncle Michael's spirit! He was in human form, huddled against the rocks, shaking in fear. Similar to engaging with our spirit guides, when encountering an entity unconnected to me, I default to asking, "Is there something I can do to help you?" His response?

"I just want to receive love."

When I asked, "By whom?", he responded, "You know who," and pointed behind me. As I shifted my gaze back into the center of the arena, my grandfather, Leslie James Benson, appeared. This wasn't a gladiator battle fortunately, no battle axes or bloodshed. In these realms, especially with experiences close to us, the bigger the emotional charge, the more help we have to ask from our guides. This is how we also activate our metacognition in this realm to release any emotions that may be driving us to become emotionally charged by our "triggers." Think of our triggers as trip wires within our subconscious, and if they are tripped, and we are still emotionally charged, then we go into trigger mode. We can do breathwork to hit the ESC and enter a higher state of consciousness, but it is much easier if this trip wire is disabled already. Just like a trap in an RPG.

By healing events within our subconscious that are triggering us, we disarm the trigger trap so that even if someone says or does something that normally triggers us, we won't react. Instead, we can observe how it normally would have triggered us, and we can find gratitude for having our consciousness back in these moments. Maybe you will get to a point where you can be curious about why the person is behaving as they are, helping them become aware of why they are acting the way they are. Unraveling our trigger loops with our family and friends is an amazing way to call in more GOUs and receive more energy in your life.

So how did I avoid being triggered at that moment? I called on Arthur to help me. As a monkey, Arthur's gift wasn't just humor and playfulness, but also a deep understanding of human emotions. I asked him, "How am I supposed to deal with this situation?" His guidance?

"Compassion is an endless well that we can draw unconditional love from."

"Become a Care Bear it is," I retorted light heartedly. Outside looking in, it probably looked pretty entertaining. It was like a *Dragon Ball Z* battle, where I was emanating waves of compassion from my heart, weathering the waves of anger and resentment spewing from my grandfather. I could feel the pull of my uncle behind me, just wanting to finally receive the love of his father.

My grandfather did love all of his children. He and my grandmother worked impossibly hard to provide for their kids and community. What my grandfather lacked was softness. And all my uncle ever wanted was to receive physical love and appreciation from his father (don't we all?).

In that moment of sending love to my grandfather, I saw that he, too, never received love that way. Growing up in Texas, fresh out of slavery, there wasn't time or space to be soft. In fact, "Being soft would get you killed," was what my father used to remind us. Leading with an open heart, would get you hung. These were their realities.

Feeling this ancestral pain, I shed tears as I continued to emanate love and light from my heart. I fell to my knees as I saw my great-great-grandfather, his great-grandfather, a chef whose hands were shot off by the shotguns of white land barons who tried to take his land. I felt the pain of past generations, of my ancestors who just bore the pain of life without healing it.

Much like the practice of Tonglen, I received the pain and sent love in return. As the waves of pain subsided, I collapsed to the ground, but my grandfather remained standing there. My uncle's spirit was relieved, and while he and my grandfather did not embrace, there was finally peace on the mountaintop.

It wasn't until the following evening that I was able to fully understand that all I had to do was cleanse myself of my pain related to my feelings of lack and insecurity. That this pain was not meant for me to wallow in, but to rejoice! To be grateful that I have my hands, I have my body, I have this beautiful mind and these incredible opportunities because of the sacrifices of the imperfect, yet dedicated, men and women that I am blessed to call my ancestors. The same, I know, goes for you.

We are living the wildest dreams of our ancestors.

Dreams dreamt of long ago, that allowed our ancestors to persevere through difficult situations, have afforded us the opportunity to activate gifts long forgotten and elevate our experiences. We get to remember that breathwork, meditation, visualization, and our imagination can heal our physical, mental, and energetic bodies. Through this healing, we not only heal ourselves in the present and future, but also our ancestral wounds from the past, for our descendants yet to come.

So, let's not let their sacrifices be in vain. Let's take the time to heal our chakras, our energy centers, so that we can call back ALL of our energy. One gem of understanding, one soul shard, one soul fragment, at a time.

BOSS MISSION 2: TRIAL OF THE SACRED CHAKRAS

This next mission is inspired by a meditation developed by Dr. Joe Dispenza. This is a similar meditation he used to heal his back and has helped others heal and upgrade their bodies as well. **The Trial of the Sacred Chakras**, a challenge that will take you on a journey with our friend Chakra the Tree, except instead of reflecting on his remembrance of wholeness, you'll be observing your own energy centers and the stories that they hold. One by one you will assess each chakra and listen to how to bring them back into harmony.

It is recommended to do this in the morning, on a day when you have at least an hour and a half to work through it. Also do not plan on drinking or intaking any substances before or afterwards that could affect your state of consciousness.

It's like going to a day spa and then eating at McDonald's afterwards. The meditation will be guided by me, accessed through our LTUVG app, and then there will be ten to fifteen minutes of journaling. Once you've successfully upgraded your avatar, hop into the "Real Life Wins!" Channel and express how you feel!

On the other side, you will gain the ability to connect with each energy center intentionally, as well as the energy around each one, having more and more awareness and control over yourself.

While observing each energy center, observe any memories that bring up lower vibrational emotions, and either say the Ho'Oponopono prayer, "I'm Sorry, Please Forgive Me, Thank You, I love you" to the memory, or this spell that works just as well:

"Thank you for helping me remember
this aspect of myself,
Your presence is no longer needed,
You must leave my world, my Universe, now!"

Remember you are sovereign and always have control over your YOUniverse, no exceptions. If there are experiences you desire to remove, remove them. There still may be what is called the "echo effect," where the changes you've made in your world now must continue to permeate through the other people in your life who are used to a different frequency signature. A teacher once referred to them as "old pictures."

For example, like my uncle, I used to fear abandonment and not being loved by the women in my life. When I saw that this experience stemmed from a breakup with a girl in fourth grade who ended up dating my older brother (who was closer to her age anyway), I was able to laugh about it and let it go. To bring this healing into my daily life, I had to give myself love in moments when I previously would act defensively. I didn't put the onus on others to show me love, I had to feel the love from within and trust it was there. If I felt I was receiving negativity or lack of care from others, I could always ask for confirmation. There also were times that if I just let the voice of doubt dissipate, others would soon show me the love that was coming all along.

It's called committing to your vibration, and this boss level is going to give you an intimate remembrance of your natural vibration. How each of your chakras, or energy centers, when cleansed, feel like.

As always, remember to have fun! This is going to systematically cleanse your body and energy and massively upgrade your V.I.S.A. so you can enjoy life, like it's the ultimate video game.

Navigate to the LTUVG App and find Boss Mission 2: Trials of the Sacred Chakras. May you be filled with acceptance, surrender, and gratitude!

Boss Mission 2 Activated

Open the LTUVG App and access Boss Mission 2:
Trials of the Sacred Chakras

Cue the fanfare! You've just completed an incredible experience where you relied on tapping into your full V.I.S.A. to surrender to listening to the subtle energy of your body, heart, and spirit. A feat that requires you to be present with yourself so that you can be in service to others through your healing process. This is an invaluable tool you should continue to practice on your own. Eventually it will allow you to do a quick scan of your energy if you ever feel "off" in any of these areas, especially after a traumatic experience. Think of this as a leveled-up version of the Spring Cleaning Meditation.

Just as you'll get to the point where you can do the centering exercise in moments, once you have a familiarity with the vibration of your chakras, you'll be able to balance them in an instant as well. Whenever I notice a shift in my energy, I take a couple deep breaths, drop into my heart space, and accept each emotion so I can transmute it into XP. Clearing the energetic clog sooner than later keeps you from losing XP during each day's challenge.

And now that you've completed this boss level, let's open your chest for your reward! And be sure to share any epiphanies you've had in the Level Up thread.

Level 9 Recap:

- Subtle Energy Skills Unlocked:
    - Intuition Controller
- Subtle Energy XP/Grinding Activities
    - Spring Cleaning Journey
    - Seed Meditation
    - Trial of the Sacred Chakras
- Universal Tools
    - 4 Most Important Questions

LEVEL 10

COURAGE THROUGH DISCOMFORT

REWARD QUEST - WELCOME YOUR COURAGEOUS COMPANION!

I am incredibly impressed by the responses and experiences that you are having with this work. The last meditation, Blessing of the Chakras, encouraged working through blockages so that you can live a life with more energy and sovereignty over yourself, which takes an incredible amount of courage. It isn't to be taken for granted, so please, give yourself so much self-love and a big hug from me.

I'm serious. Right now, stop reading, and give yourself a big hug from me. If that makes you uncomfortable, I'm sorry, but then you need to give yourself a hug twice as long. As we know by now, love is healing. If there is discomfort around it, then it probably means that when you were working through the heart space, it was harder for you to focus and/or receive messages. That's okay!

I once had a lot of deficiencies in my heart space, which affected my voice and ability to honor the love that I wanted to give to the world. I mentioned earlier about my soul retrieval experiences with Itzhak, in that Zai'Ra and I both had incredibly healing experiences with him. At this moment, I'm going to share my first journey with Itzhak, because you are finally going to meet your sacred spirit animal!

This is your reward for completing the Boss Activity, so if you are reading ahead, stop, go back, and do the Blessing of the Chakras meditation. No freebies! Again, this book is designed to efficiently bring all of your abilities online, and if you skip anything, especially the boss levels, you will be missing out on the necessary experience points to access the more transformational tools.

For all those who have completed the prerequisites, this is your reward. This is your first opportunity to bring the spirit avatar from our first quest into the physical realm! But also, be open to the animal being different, it's only your inner knowing that will guide you to the appropriate animal for you. You may have more; this may just be the first one that you meet.

You remember Arthur, my companion who supported me at the Shadow Mountain levels within my subconscious? Well, he was not the first spirit animal that I gained. The first that I gained was actually a red-tailed hawk named Athena, and she came to me so I could remember how to fly.

So, jump into the LTUVG app, and let's remember to fly together!

Reward Mission Activated
Open the LTUVG App and access Reward Mission:
Welcome Your Courageous Companion

What spirit animal came to you? Was it the same animal as your spirit avatar? Was it different? A lion, tiger, or bear (oh my)? In this situation, these are your friends, so no need to be afraid. These divine friends are here to support you. After you connect with your power animal, remember to journal, to remember the journey.

Just like our Sacred Heart Sanctuary journey, remembering these details will serve you in further connection with your SSA and IRR. Just like anything else, the more you enter this space, the more vivid the realm will become. The more opportunities that you get to level up your imagination the more they will speed up the manifestation of your dreams. Your SSA also has its own skill tree that you want to build up as well. I'll cover my experience with this in the upcoming book, but for now, the more you visualize your SSA, the more you'll learn about them.

Michael Jordan said that before he ever made the game-winning shot, he visualized it 100 times. By connecting with your Imagination Realization Realm and your new spirit guide, you'll earn valuable XP that will benefit you in the present and future. What if you want to earn XP directly in the physical realm with your SSA? Then I'd find a totem that reminds you of that spirit animal. Like Leonardo DiCaprio's spinning top in *Inception*, it will act as a reminder for you. A reminder to embody the essence of this power animal, whenever the time calls for it.

For Athena, my red-tailed hawk, I found a small stone carving of a hawk that I would keep with me at first, and then on my altar that I would connect with every morning. Whenever I had a moment in life where fear would creep in, I would ask Athena if she could support me in maintaining my courage under fire. Another amazing tool is to either google or look up your spirit animal in *The Shaman's Guide to Power Animals*.

Just like in *Zelda: Breath of the Wild* where you build a relationship with your horse by giving them love, the more that you connect with your power animal, the stronger that bond will become. As that bond becomes stronger, the power level of your spirit animal will increase, which will also increase your own ability to connect with other SSAs depending on what type of challenges come to you.

Over time, after building a strong relationship with Athena, I soon connected with Fern, my deer who I chased after on my first journey! Yes, she actually was my first spirit animal in life, representing my gentle nature. I wasn't meant to talk to her on that journey, I needed to meet Athena so that I could let go of fear.

Then came Arthur, the monkey who helped me through the Shadow Mountain stage, and Grant, my black panther, who I just spent 13 hours getting permanently canonized on my back. You'll learn more about Grant in the future, he's a badass. A gentle badass, but a badass all the same.

Each SSA appears at different moments on our life's quest, depending on what types of challenges we are facing. Each spirit animal is an aspect of our own divine nature and will support us intuitively on our journey back to ourselves.

So don't hesitate to call on your Sacred Spirit Animal, ask what name they prefer to be called, and how they can best support you. Because it's all about collecting those GOUs, soul shards, and soul fragments of your whole self. You've come so far on your journey, and you're only a couple of levels away from finishing this arc of your awakening quest, keep going.

Level 10 Recap:

- Subtle Energy XP/Grinding Activities
    - Transformational Sacred Spirit Animal Breathquest
- Universal Tools Acquired
    - Sacred Spirit Animal (SSA)

LEVEL 11

CONVICTION, THE WIND BENEATH OUR BELIEFS

QUEST 21: SUMMONING YOUR DIVINE GUARDIAN COUNSEL

Remember when I asked you early on in this journey to suspend your disbelief in what you think you know about this reality, or this "game of life" as I love to put it? If you have made it this far in the journey, thank you for trusting me, and for trusting your intuition and your inner knowing. By now you should be comfortable with some of your practices.

Maybe some of you are even able to drop into your HMC technique by closing your eyes and counting down from 3,2,1 and hitting the ESC button to drop into alpha or theta mode. Maybe you're connecting with your higher self and your SSA to support the challenges in your day. If you are still working on getting there, keep practicing! Keep raising your awareness to the messages from the world around you. It is trying to give you hints of the subtle realm that is alive and thriving around you.

In this chapter, we will cover the sixth and "final" Universal Principle, Conviction. This principle explains why I asked you to suspend your disbelief. Your belief system can either boost your sails to reach your dreams, or deflate them.

By suspending your disbelief, you created room for your experience to inform you of what is possible. You allowed new neural networks to determine what is real, and what is an illusion. This is why some of you are living a much different life, while others might still be struggling. As I've stated in many of our missions, this is perfectly normal. Especially for you highly stubborn analytical individuals. I can say this because I was one of them. It's why I have weaved scientific evidence, clinical studies, and quantum theories to support each mission.

Whether you are picking this up quickly or taking more time, be patient and compassionate with yourselves. The most important thing to remember is that you are EXACTLY where you are supposed to be on your healing journey. Keep practicing, and your skills will keep activating.

I heard this story about Thomas Edison, an incredible inventor in the late 1800's, and it truly inspired me. He was not considered a prodigy when he was a child, not even close. In school, he was considered "addled" by his teachers before his mom pulled him out of school. For those googling the word addled, it means "unable to think clearly." Thomas never knew why his mom pulled him out of school; he just knew that she believed in him with all of her heart.

"My mother was the making of me.
She was so true, so sure of me, and I
felt I had someone to live for,
someone I must not disappoint."

Thomas Edison later reflected. When he was a young man and his mom passed away, he worked his hardest to make her proud. His conviction in this led him to become one of the best inventors of our time.

What would have happened if his mom had not believed in him? Maybe he makes it to the same place, but more often we see kids and adults alike reach the heights of the expectations of others. To avoid the pain of disappointment, we stay safe within the bounds of others' limiting beliefs, which then become our own.

This Universal Principle of Conviction asks you to slowly reengage your faith in what you've been experiencing and to let go of any previous limiting beliefs based on past experiences. The final level of this book, what we've been building toward to rescue your soul shard, will take you to a place to let go of a limiting belief (or many) in return for your inner child. When you get there, it will be a beautiful quest. And to get there, you must build your conviction in this new way of living (or playing the game of life).

As a football-playing mechanical engineer from Princeton, I too, had to let go of many limiting beliefs anchored in Western science. I wouldn't believe in anything unless I could study it, prove it in a theorem, or experience it. It wasn't until I experienced plant medicine, or shrooms, in a social setting that I began to believe in the magic of the subtle realm.

By the time this experience happened, I already had my first sacred spirit animal, but I was "taking a break" from spiritualism. I was living a fairly unconscious life while building my wealth in finance. It feels like a lifetime ago because music is such a big part of my life now, but back then, it was completely blocked from me. This is how I unlocked that skill tree within me.

I went to a friend's home in the woods up in Vermont, where I met his DJ buddy, Harrison. When I got to the house and gave Harrison a hug, we started talking about music and life. I realized we could have been brothers. He also happened to be a very talented DJ, and I said I wanted to learn from him if he had time that weekend. An open book, he obliged to teach me while he was mixing music. One thing led to another, and before I knew it, we all had ingested some magic mushrooms and started roaming outside. It's slowly coming back to me like a lucid dream.

At the pinnacle of the experience, I was in the forest, where I could still hear the music Harrison was playing from the house. Every time I closed my eyes, I saw these large beams of light coming out of the ground. When I opened my eyes, all I saw were these big trees. As I opened and closed my eyes, I realized that the lights were the trees! I closed my eyes again, and like Neo after he lost his sight in *The Matrix*, I followed the lights until I got to the largest beam. With nervous courage, I approached the ominous light. It was buzzing with exciting electricity. I got so close I could sense the warmth of the electricity putting the edges of my arm hairs on full alert. Should I touch it?

Ziiiiiing. My hand connected to the beam of light like a magnet, and my soul was instantaneously transported into the center of the earth and the center of my Universe simultaneously. As soon as I was in this place, my soul was transported back into my body. "Whoa," I remember saying, as smoke came out of my ears because I was so wowed by this experience. The next thing I remember hearing after the smoke settled was Harrison's music from the house. I immediately wandered back to the house and began learning how to DJ from him.

On the drive home, listening to music was a whole new experience. I would hear one song and immediately hear two or three other songs that would mix with it in my head. I later learned that what unlocked within me was the ability to harmonize by ear and have a sensory recall of what song matched that pitch from my inner music catalog. I now DJ on a radio station weekly, love the music I create, which exemplifies the interconnectedness of all music. One major highlight was during COVID, I put together online music festivals with 50 artists worldwide to raise awareness for voting rights. We helped get thousands to the polls that day and had fun while doing it.

My music continues to uplift others, and it was this experience that helped me remember it was a part of my purpose.

How does this relate to my conviction that the subtle energy realm is real? It was when this memory was illustrated by an oracle in front of my eyes.

Fast forward five or six years, when Zai'Ra and I took our journey into Mordor. In the third or fourth ceremony with Shar, I was advised to let go of music in this journey. "Let go of music?!" I internally reacted. Turns out, I had a lot of ego tied up in my gift of music. I had to know, was music my purpose, or a projection of my ego. The only way to know for sure, was to let it go. Much like the Mariah Carey song, if it's meant to be, it will come back to me.

I'll spare all the details of the journey, except to say that after this experience, I fully accepted that "randomness" is the door the Universe uses to communicate with us, and that there are NO coincidences. I trust in this so much that I believe if you maintain an open mind, you will be convinced of the same thing.

How did this occur? At the beginning and end of every ceremony, we would pull oracle cards from the Gaia deck. I sit with oracle cards daily now, but in the beginning, every time I pulled a card, there would be this little voice of fear, doubting which card to choose. The beginning of the journey I pulled a card called Night Wind which stood for "facing fear, subconscious release, healing." It was perfect for this journey, because I indeed faced my fear to the question of "what am I without music?" And as I dissolved this fear into a pool of unconditional love for my true self, I heard music erupting from within the depths of my heart. Music is a part of me, and I'm a part of it! I closed the journey with my heart vibrating with a blissful light.

In the morning after we shared our experiences, Shar walked around for us to pull an oracle card to close the journey. I was nervous. Frankly I didn't want to pull a card after that amazing journey.

"What if the card I pull shows me something contrary to my journey?" "What if my ego is showing me what I want to see? And music actually isn't a part of my purpose?" I could feel fear and doubt attempting to infiltrate my thoughts.

Then I heard a voice, "Whatever card you pull will be the perfect card for you." In that instant, my fear melted away. My journey was my journey; trust it! With that, I pulled the card that felt right without a second thought. This book is not a picture book, but I am putting a picture here for impact. When I turned the card over, it literally depicted the scene of my first journey with mushrooms. The card was "Intuitive Communication," showing a woman (intuition) connecting with the heart of a tree in the forest.

Silent whispers of the heart, this card "confirmed that [I] have natural psychic ability that can be further developed and explained... [you are] one with all creation. All is energetically connected..." These explanations, plus this photo below, illustrated and described my experience of connecting energetically with the source of creation (through the tree & Mother Earth) and activating my natural psychic ability.

Tears began streaming down my face, as I surrendered in that moment to the intuitive guidance of the Universe. To my own inner knowing.

MISSION 21: DIVINE GUARDIAN COUNSEL ACTIVATION

"The Universe never misses."

This is a quote that I live by, because of the crazy "coincidences" that have guided Zai'Ra and I since our journey into and out of Mordor. The Universe's communication with us through "randomness" is one of the best video games I've ever played, and when it communicates with you, you'll feel the same way.

If you have stories to share, please drop them in the "Gratitude Lobby" Channel in the LTUVG app. It will serve to help others on their own journey to build their own conviction in the Universe and their own supernatural powers.

"Synchronicities are the jokers in nature's pack of cards, for they refuse to play by the rules and offer a hint that, in our quest for certainty about the Universe, we may have ignored some vital clues."

This quote by renowned physicist and author, F. David Peat, certainly supports this idea of coincidences. But there is more to this quest. With your conviction activated—your next step is to activate your own counsel to receive additional guidance from the Universe.

Go to the LTUVG app, and we'll finish this epic story and activate your last ability.

Mission 21 Activated

Open the LTUVG App and access Mission 21:
Divine Guardian Counsel Activation

Amazing! You have your full gambit of tools to practice your skills and fully activate your V.I.S.A. Let's take a moment and give honor to the accomplishment that you've made. Head back to the app and review the 6Cs of Universal Principles in the "Ascended Players' Hub" Channel and how they all support one another.

You'll also find additional challenges and updated prompts in this Circle now that you've finished Level 10. You are officially a **Life Gamer Adept**!

End Game Content Activated
Open the LTUVG App and complete Level 11 to gain access to the "Ascended Players Hub" channel for end game content.

Level 11 Recap:

- Universal Tools Acquired
    - Divine Guardian Counsel

LEVEL 12

JUMPING BACK INTO THE GAME OF LIFE!

BACK INTO THE FIRE

Remember I promised that I would share how we made it back from Mordor, and our fool's errand to "save our world"? Well, we've made it to that part of the book. But first, let's take a moment to reflect on the courageous journey you have taken! We must commemorate this moment as a graduation from practice mode.

If you've been journaling this adventure, take a page and mark the date, and write a few reasons why you are grateful for yourself and the skills that you have developed on this journey. Also go to the LGG community and write: "I've graduated!" in the "Commitment Forge" Channel. Add one or more things you're grateful for about this journey.

Graduating from practice mode means you've probably also been living a lot of real life while working through this manifesto. The truth is that there isn't really a "practice mode" in life. Every day is an opportunity to grow and be deeply present with the challenges of our lives; the difference is the consequences of not using the skills at our disposal. Life, like many video games, gives us multiple chances to integrate the lessons it tries to teach us. However, if we don't listen, the consequences can get gradually more drastic. Take a moment to think about moments in your life where this is true.

For Zai'Ra and me, even though we did walk through Mordor to try to "save our world," the Universe smiled upon us with the support we needed to escape this treacherous world with our lives. We paid quite a hefty price, but the wisdom and gifts of remembering ourselves and helping others heal from deep trauma was well worth it. Speaking of, let's jump back into this tumultuous journey to the heart of the fiery mountain of Mordor.

When we last left off, it was fall of 2020. We had started The Warrior Sanctuary and agreed to partner with Shar and help support her ceremonies with the intention of building a healing community. We accomplished this by leasing a townhouse in Manhattan that we turned into a healing center, and where we held the healing ceremonies. Retreats were held weekly for the first five months, a deep and intense study of what being in service to the community was during COVID.

The purpose of creating The Warrior Sanctuary was to create a bridge for individuals looking for ancestral healing while creating sustainability for the organization. Our partnership with Shar was the "pilot program." For every ceremony, a small percentage of the ceremony fee would be made to our organization as a donation. Our agreement was simple, we leased the space, she held the ceremonies, and together we would create healing for a lot of people. We just had to help her move out of her loft and into our space first. Key word, JUST.

Moving day morning came, and I still remember how quickly our joy and excitement melted into confusion and despair as we entered her apartment. We saw what hoarding looks like in a New York City apartment—bathtubs as storage lockers, expert use of space saver bags, and two storage units we didn't know about! Needless to say, we were unaware of just how much baggage she came with—literally and soon to be figuratively.

As we were processing the size of the move and questioning the ship we were about to sail away on, we also were confronted with her disintegrating romantic relationship. The explosive drama between her and her partner was fraught with fear, deceit, suicidal threats and belligerent aggression indicating deeper mental health issues.

Later that night, after a "successful move" Zai'Ra and I were strategizing on how to get out of the lease, but we were stuck. "We got duped," was our conclusion, but we hoped that our beautiful healing work would help us all become the best versions of ourselves. Unsurprisingly, for the rest of the summer, fall, and winter, it only got worse. We supported Shar through what felt like an MTV reality TV show; delusional enough to think that it would get better.

For about seven months this was the cycle: hosting a beautiful ceremony over the weekend, drama exploding Monday, Zai'Ra and I supporting and cleaning up the mess; by the middle of the week, things were stabilizing; by Thursday/Friday, we were rushing to get ready to host another ceremony. What held this chaos together? The fact that our friends and family were having transformational healing experiences of life-long trauma.

One of our dear friends healed from her mother's tragic passing and a bout with cancer. Through her healing, she has reengaged with her music career and is charting around the world with an incredible single. Her breakthrough transformation and reclamation of her own healing power happened in that ceremony space. Every weekend there were miracles of the healing power of love happening within individuals, and it was profound and magical—especially during a time when so many people were suffering from grief and loss.

What undermined this beautiful work was the lack of donations after each ceremony. During those months where we held over 50 ceremonies, Shar never donated anything to The Warrior Sanctuary. She always had a reason she couldn't donate, and we always forgave her debts, at first. Eventually Zai'Ra and I realized that to be on our highest path, integrity cannot be sacrificed. Not in the slightest.

How did this saga end? Would Zai and I finally see that this "gift" could not be wielded by anyone? That it must be thrown back into the fire from whence it was forged? We'll see.

Around March of 2021, we had a big retreat planned. A Healing Retreat for Healers. We had secured an entire campus of an artist's residency upstate and had invited some incredibly talented healers to work together to co-create a retreat to manifest a portal of transformation with our gifts combined. Unfortunately, we did have to tap into our deepest healing powers to protect our friends from our misguided shaman.

By this time, Shar was drained of energy from her constant internal and external conflicts. A word to the wise, when a person is at a deficit and is desperate, the desire to survive can create a dangerous environment for everyone involved. Avoid putting them and yourself in these situations.

While our group of "healers" came with good intentions, it also created an unintentional environment of competition and ego for Shar. This created the opportunity for negative polarity to attach to her. Fear, panic, anxiety and unresolved traumas of the past and present all wickedly danced in the room together, forcing us to quite literally face the music.

During the ceremony, as the music played and the medicine worked its way through the room, we all were compelled to face the darkness. To see the true demons of those we were working with. This ceremony felt like the ultimate boss level, with protective wards being thrown, the joker's laughter, the swindler's hex, triumphant hero's and a destructive fallout.

In this "final battle" we were victorious, but everyone lost. Lines were crossed and it cast a brutal look at the agreements we had entered into—we had to end it and end it now. We had very naively opened a channel of energy without truly understanding duality and the laws of the Universe. Not one Universal Law says that you must use your powers for good for them to work. And Shar was using her powers for service to self, holding negative polarity. It was at that moment that we knew we had to break ties with her. She had to be thrown in the fires of Mordor (not literally, to be clear). But how?

That night we realized she had been one of our biggest teachers. We had given away our power and blindly followed a person who ultimately wasn't aligned with our values. She reflected our weak spots: codependency, savior complex, not being willing to speak up for ourselves, ego, fear of abandonment, and fear of admitting a mistake. That was the darkness we experienced that night; our own fears and the power one can wield when there are imbalances in our awareness equilibrium.

There was a lot of fear surrounding this breakup because there were so many connections that needed to be severed. How would we walk ourselves out of this without damaging the community who believed in the illusory beauty of what we've created? How would we cut ties cleanly and ask Shar to leave The Warrior Sanctuary? If she moved out, how were we going to pay rent? Should we just take the entire loss? $200k down the drain? We needed guidance.

A VISIT TO THE ORACLE

There is a dear friend we met along our journeys who we refer to as "The Oracle." She utilizes divination, oracle and tarot cards to communicate between her and her clients' Divine guides to answer any questions her clients have. We met her through our Reiki class before this whole adventure started. She was the only person we could rely on because she hadn't been involved in any of our ceremonies.

The special thing about the Oracle is that she only wants to know your question, and nothing else. This way, when her guidance aligns with the rest of the situation, her clients will take the guidance more seriously.

When we finally received our appointment with the Oracle, we knew what question to ask. It was simple.

"How do we navigate out of a difficult business partnership with the least damage possible to everyone involved?"

By the end of our session, she was SO accurate with the assessment of the situation, we swore she was our confidant throughout the entire adventure!

She channeled that we were dealing with a "trickster" who had been fooling us since the beginning. Not to say that a "trickster" is inherently bad, these are archetypes found across cultures and historical lores globally and often serve as very valuable human relating experiences. The point was, she had deceived us from the beginning. This probably hurt the most because, even from the beginning, it seemed Shar planned to use us for her benefit.

This is why I am eternally grateful. Because while she thought she was using us, the Universe was using her as a tool, for Zai'Ra and I to awaken fully. And the price of that gift? Again, it is priceless.

The Oracle advised us to cut ties immediately, and without emotions. And by severing this tie cleanly, we were advised that the relationship would end swiftly and without repercussions, creating space for abundance and authentic teachers on the other side. The last part was very important for us, that a lot of abundance would be waiting for us, really grounded us in throwing the ring back into the fire (again, not literally).

Soon the day came. We were scheduled to have a zoom call to talk about "future projects." Boy, was she surprised when we, without emotion, said that we were dissolving the partnership. We made it about needing to spend time nourishing our relationship, that we had lost ourselves in running retreats.

At first, she was shocked and tried to manipulate the situation. But we stayed firm and didn't give any emotional energy to the situation. We thanked her for the lessons she had taught us and further explained that we weren't getting the abundance we needed to continue supporting the ceremonies. We also needed to focus on our relationship and wedding! We needed our own joy back in our life, which was very true. Zai'Ra and my relationship experienced its most difficult challenges during this journey, and the last thing we wanted was to lose the Divine Love we had for one another in the process.

After some time, and negotiations on how long she needed before moving out, that was it. Just like that, the ring was tossed into the fire, and Shar was out of our lives. Quite literally, the day we broke ties with her, two teachers came into our lives. One that taught me the ancient healing arts of Tibetan Sound Healing, and another that taught Zai'Ra the magical skill of Pravada Sound Healing with flutes and sound bridging.

A tale for another time, but we also were married by an ancient tribe of Ecuador! We soon found land to build a retreat there AND received funding for that as well! Since then, we've been building an authentic and beautiful community there (Amaroo) with Itzhak Beery, who hosts the same shamanism apprenticeship there every January. The same apprenticeship program that Zai'Ra and I took, all those years ago.

We were blessed to have this tumultuous experience serve as the practice mode for us. For even though the game we entered was indeed dangerous, Shar didn't mean us ill will, she just wanted to be famous.

"If you ever work with a healer who wants to be famous, politely decline."

This was the advice Itzhak gave us after we shared our tale with him.

Why am I sharing this particular story at this moment? Because you now have a ton of gifts and skills at your disposal to tap into the subtle energy realm. Discernment is crucial in navigating the subtle energy realm. If you haven't gotten an oracle deck yet, certainly invest in one or two, and start to use it as a medium to connect with your council as you ask for guidance.

One deck that was incredible for us in the beginning was the Sacred Animal Oracle deck. Something accessible as we all know what a lion, tiger, or eagle reminds us of. This can also help build a relationship with more spirit animals. If you want to gain valuable XP for your intuition, I highly recommend doing this. Get a deck, cleanse it, and every morning ask the question,

***"What energy supports my highest vibrational path today,
For the good of myself and everyone involved?"***

Then pull a card every day and see how embodying the energy of that card impacts your day. It's changed my life for the better. At worst, this practice will make you more present, gaining XP for your Awareness as well as your Intuition. Remember our goal is to stack XP whenever we can. In addition, it will help with discernment when encountering new characters in the game of life.

Always be curious about people's intentions to understand what they want to get out of any situation, especially if money is involved. If relationships aren't flowing, then don't fight against the current or sacrifice your principles you just learned in order to maintain these relationships.

Lean on your **4 Most Important Questions** as a guide map. In fact, if you are doing the work, then most likely some relationships will be cut away, sometimes very abruptly. While painful, it is a good sign that you are on your highest path. Don't be righteous about it, just observe that it's happening.

A quick note that is important before we close the first arc of this awakening process. I will cover the Universal Laws that uphold the Universal Principles in future books to come, but to help with your growth process, let's dive a little into one of those laws: The Law of Vibration.

Most people know the Law of Attraction, a philosophical concept that states that individuals can attract positive or negative experiences based on the energy, thoughts, and feelings they put out into their YOUniverse.[68] The Law of Vibration explains why the Law of Attraction works. When you hold a thought, it emits a vibration, vibrations are frequencies which carry information.

---

[68] Proctor, B. (2011). The ABCs of Success: The Essential Principles from America's Greatest Prosperity Teacher. Tarcher Perigee.

According to these laws, by aligning your vibrations (thoughts and emotions) with the frequency of what you desire, you can attract those things into your life.

"The quantum field doesn't respond to what you want. It responds to what you are being."[69]

Utilizing these laws, be conscious of which of the 6Cs you are calling in. Trusting that if it's for your highest purpose, it will flow to you. If you feel the need to "chase" something, then it is highly likely it is of the ego or mind space. Reaching out to grab it is one thing, chasing it down is another. Let our journey to Mordor be a lesson for you.

To help you remember all the amazing skills that you unlocked, don't forget to lean on the Skill Codex section in the LTUVG App. You can now access the Skill Codex IV preparing you for the endgame.

SAVE POINT 5: WARNING! THE LAST SAVE POINT

Have you ever played an RPG like Final Fantasy or Baldur's Gate where, near the end of the game, you'll receive a message like this:

Warning: Beyond this point, you cannot save. Ensure you are prepared before continuing.

[69] Lipton, B. H. (2005). The Biology of Belief: Unleashing the Power of Consciousness, Matter & Miracles. Mountain of Love Productions.

This message lets you know that you're about to enter the final dungeon. Which means you are now at that part of this book, and while there technically won't be a point of "no return," when you decide to enter the castle where your inner child is, you won't be able to stop the journey. It will be a 90 minute breathquest to rescue your inner child. Once you start it, there is no stopping it, so you want to make sure that you've cleared away as much debris from your subconscious as possible. In addition, you want to be sure you've leveled up your summons, guides and skillset to ensure the deepest and most complete reunion possible.

If you attempt the rescue and fall short of the intention you set at the beginning of this book, of course you can always attempt the breathquest again; just like attempting to beat a game multiple times. But that isn't necessary for most people. Most of my students who have prepared for this journey experience a full reunion in one session. And I want that outcome for you as well.

At a minimum, you should be practicing breathwork, meditation, and visualization five minutes a day. 15 minutes is obviously much better, and my best students have 30 minutes of daily practices so they can rescue their inner child and live the life of their dreams sooner than later.

For myself, after three years of consistent daily practice, I can drop into journey space and/or meditation space in an instant, and soon, you will be able do the same thing!

To get a full refresher of all the amazing skills and abilities you've collected over the course of this epic adventure, as well as assess the levels of your V.I.S.A. and all your 6Cs of Universal Principles, drop into your trusty LTUVG app for your *FINAL SAVE POINT.* Once you feel confident in your abilities, continue into the final level where you will attempt the Rite of Ascension Challenge to test your wisdom of the content of the book and gain the key to the castle holding your inner child.

Good luck!

! Save Point 5: !

Warning! The Last Save Point Unlocked
Go to LTUVG App

LEVEL 13

THE END GAME & BEYOND

Just as at the end of *LOTR*, I must part ways with you and leave middle earth, your lower realm, for you to honor and defend. This is your End Game. You have the tools, just continue using them and listening to your higher self. Just be present. Life Gamer's let the game come to them and then respond. Follow that mantra, and you can never lose.

I am excited for you to grow and blossom in your new awareness of Universal Attributes, skills and abilities that you've unlocked. Remember to continually assess your V.I.S.A. and try to stretch your skill set by increasingly grinding to improve the skill trees of the 6Cs of Universal Principles. Don't forget that you have a community to build and connect with along your journey. I will also be providing updates on how I'll be supporting you live as well in the LTUVG app, so stay tuned!

The possibilities that you will reach are only limited by your ability to shift your perspective of each challenge in your day. Utilizing your presence and creativity to reframe your problems, making use of your HMC technique and hitting the ESC button when needed to observe why an event is happening.

I can't tell you what the next part of your journey will look like, but I can say that it will most certainly challenge your areas of "weakness" if you choose to lean into the discomfort of transformation. Just like in *Skyrim* or any amazing RPG, as we build up our character, so will our challenges build up. If you want to attain the most experience points, then it will require you to show up to the biggest challenges.

"It is only in the edges of discomfort that we discover a deeper level of connection with ourselves and our world around us."

Remember to get 1 percent better every day and you'll be 37 times better in a year, 1400 times better in just two years! So, log in daily to get your XP bonus. Periodically check in on your V.I.S.A. Skill Assessment to see how you've leveled up each area.

Build out your "gaming sanctuary" with your cleansing agents and over time maybe invest in some crystals. Crystals have been used for centuries to cleanse and amplify our natural abilities. There is a reason why games have them in weapons and armor. I highly recommend getting the book *Understanding Crystals.*

And when you are ready, there is one final mission to complete. We have to rescue our inner child! But first, I need to know that you are ready for this level. The last thing we want is to take on this level and not be ready to let go of the limiting beliefs keeping us from this reunion.

In service to your inner child, there is a Rite of Passage that you must go through to unlock access to the Final Boss Quest;

The **Transformational Breathquest to Rescue You Inner Child**.

Think of it as a version of "The Proving" from Horizon Zero Dawn, a badge of ascension to tap into your inner genius and unlock a treasure trove of abilities within you.

So what are you waiting for?!? Your inner child is beckoning for your help!

Go to the Rite of Ascension Challenge in the LTUVG app and complete the trials. These trials will test your knowledge of the skills and abilities of this book, and when you "pass" the trials, you will receive your Rite of Ascension Badge, which **unlocks** the Final Boss Mission, of this adventure, the **Transformative Breathquest to Rescue Your Inner Child**.

🏰 **Final Boss Mission Activation** 🏰

Open the LTUVG App and complete the *Rite of Ascension Challenge* to Unlock the ***Final Boss – the Transformative Breathquest to Rescue Your Inner Child***'

Congratulations! Which is an understatement of the courage, compassion, creativity, clarity, and consistent conviction that you have shown toward your healing journey. This reunion with your inner child has sent shockwaves of transformation in your past and into the future. Much like the scene where Neo integrated his wisdom and knowledge of being able to control all aspects of his experience, these waves will take time to settle into your own reality.

To keep it simple, the key for the next twenty-four or forty-eight hours is to be gentle with yourself. As indicated in the journey, please make sure you journal the experience so that you can return to it. It's something that I returned to for years afterward in order to create the depth of remembrance needed. Think of it as being able to replay a level in a video game, where you'll extract more XP from the level in your memory. If we are able to relive it in our minds, we are able to relive it in our bodies and gain more "aha" moments, and maybe even extract another GOU and maybe even another soul fragment.

Another key aspect for maintaining and building our relationship with our inner child is to acquire something in this physical realm that can remind you of that promise you made during the journey. Much like the totem for your spirit animal, find something that reminds you to honor and keep your inner child sacred.

For you are not your traumas, they are
simply breadcrumbs, mirrors,
Guiding you back to who you are, t
o who you always have been.

LEVEL 14

WHAT'S IN THE BEYOND

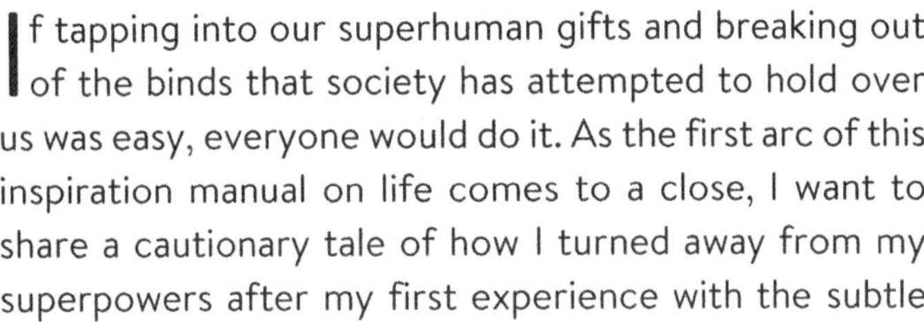

If tapping into our superhuman gifts and breaking out of the binds that society has attempted to hold over us was easy, everyone would do it. As the first arc of this inspiration manual on life comes to a close, I want to share a cautionary tale of how I turned away from my superpowers after my first experience with the subtle energy realm.

After earning my sacred spirit animals and creating my sacred heart space, I avoided doing the hard levels. I remembered that I could fly but never ventured toward Shadow Mountain. As a result, the pain that I was avoiding manifested itself in my life and hurt innocent people. If I could have learned these lessons earlier, it would have prevented more trauma occurring. I'm a firm believer that life doesn't give us challenges that we aren't ready to overcome. But we still have to make the choice to hit "start" on those levels and do "the work."

Imagine how long it would take to beat an RPG where you need to be level 100 to defeat the final boss, but you only practice clearing level 5 dungeons. How many extra hours of gaming would it take you to eventually reach level 100? In life, unlike gaming, you do have a finite number of years to clear these levels before time expires. This is why, if we ignore the more difficult levels that life is asking us to clear, more intense dis-ease and trauma will pop up in your life to raise your awareness to "the work" that you need to do.

It's like an imaginary timer in the background of our lives that, over time, increases the difficulty of our experiences. Even if we shut ourselves inside to protect ourselves from the chaos of our lives, it will show up as an autoimmune dis-ease, chronic illnesses, or sometimes worse.

To close this chapter in your evolution, I will share a miraculous story that will hopefully inspire you to apply the practices we've learned together more and more, each day you plug into the game of life.

In Level 3, I shared a story of how Zai'Ra lived with a type of lupus autoimmune disease with no known cures. After we journeyed together to hold the pain from this disease at bay, I alluded that she would eventually heal herself. This is the miraculous story of how she found out she was healed.

One day, years after that initial journey, after we had opened The Warrior Sanctuary and held many plant medicine ceremonies, healing from our ancestral wounds, Zai'Ra said to me, "I don't have lupus anymore."

I paused, thinking maybe it was how she was feeling at that moment, and she was trying to manifest it healing in her body.

"You mean you don't feel affected by it?" I asked.

"No, it's gone," she repeated.

"How do you know?" I asked inquisitively with a twinge of doubt.

"I've been off the medication for a while, and I feel amazing!" she exclaimed. "And I checked in with my guides, and they confirmed that it is gone."

Shocked, but also trusting her intuition, I responded, "If it's gone, then we should get a test to confirm it's gone."

I fully believed that when she got tested it would come back negative. I also wanted to be sure because I was concerned about blood clots popping up since she was no longer taking the blood thinners. Unfortunately, she didn't make time to go. Years went by without any flare-ups, until...

Until one day, as she was playing with our cat Samson, she knocked her head on a bench, giving herself a nasty concussion. It was so debilitating that she had to take a few weeks off work, lying still in pure darkness while I gave her Reiki. As soon as she felt better, we had to hop on a flight for a work trip. On the flight home, her calf started to hurt, and she started getting specks of blood popping up on the inside of her arms. Disconcerted, she informed me that these physical symptoms were tell-tale signs of blood clots.

Trying not to freak out, as soon as we landed, we headed to the hospital. Shocked, the doctors were livid that she had been off her meds for years. However, as they scanned her body with the ultrasound machine, they found ZERO blood clots in her body. She was as shocked as the doctors, so much that she asked for the ultrasound gun herself. Again, no blood clots. Just for confirmation, they took her blood to ensure that she still had lupus (again, a disease with no known cures).

On our ride home, she and I were perplexed by what had just transpired. The part that was most confusing was that the physical symptoms also disappeared from her body after they found no clots.

Coincidentally, I had just been studying the power of the mind, and how it can create what are called "phantom pains." This is when amputees feel pain in limbs that they no longer have. It's a condition that is well documented, but not well explained.[70] In the case of Zai'Ra, I hypothesized that this could also happen with diseases that the body has healed from energetically without physical evidence.

For example, when someone has lupus, if they are inactive for prolonged periods of time and then change the pressure in their body (like being on a flight), that is a fertile environment for a blood clot to occur. I reasoned that because her body still thought it had lupus, it manifested the symptoms of a blood clot. This is all assuming that the lupus was gone. So, we waited

---

[70] Ramachandran, V. S., & Blakeslee, S. (1998). Phantoms in the Brain: Probing the Mysteries of the Human Mind. William Morrow.

with bated breath for the results to come in with an open mind.

2 long weeks later, we got the results. She opened the letter and slowly read the results.

“So, what does it say?” I eagerly asked.

“Guess what?” She asked with a tinge of excitement.

“It’s gone?!?”

“It’s GONE!” She exclaimed!

I looked at the results myself, I couldn’t believe it, even after all the miracles we’d experienced, this was the first medical miracle I’d ever seen in person. Her lupus was indeed gone! Another freakin’ miracle! A disease that Western medicine has no cure for, her body had cured. Through healing her ancestral wounds with her parents[71], with whom she has a loving relationship now, her body was able to let go of the energy that was attacking her central nervous system and blood.[72] It’s one of those experiences that inspires us to not only continue doing the work but encourage others to do the same for them.

What does this mean for you?

My chief editor, aka Mom, advised that I remind you that this does NOT mean to ignore your doctors’ instructions

[71] Wolynn, M. (2016). It Didn't Start with You: How Inherited Family Trauma Shapes Who We Are and How to End the Cycle.
[72] Pert, C. B. (1997). Molecules of Emotion: Why You Feel the Way You Feel.

and go off your medications. Especially if you have an illness you are healing from, listen to your doctor.

It does mean that as complicated challenges in your life come up, just like in a video game, go into your toolbox and utilize a breathwork exercise, tap into a visualization like the Imagination Realization Realm Technique, call on the guidance of your spirit animal or guardian counsel, and see each challenge as a level you can clear! While balancing out "real world" fears, make sure you are also utilizing the gifts you were born with to navigate the challenge. Because, as always:

Life isn't happening TO you,
Life is happening FOR you,
to learn from, and level up.

If you fall out of your practices, remember compassion, and get back on the wagon. You also have a growing community to connect with, you are never alone on your journey. And I'm always here for support. Lean into the app for references and the Tzolkin calendar, and oracle cards as well. You are never alone on your journey.

Congratulate yourself for taking a huge leap into the unknown and taking control of your life, so that you can enjoy it, as you would your favorite video game. Reframing life's problems into levels that, once you clear, provide you with gems of understanding to level up your life. Keep up the progress, and I will see you soon to help you upgrade from a Life Gamer to an Ascension Gamer.

Until then, sending you positive energy of curiosity, consistency, compassion, creativity, clarity, courage, and conviction, for your continued, leveling-up process.

See you soon.

Made in the USA
Coppell, TX
30 January 2026

70527048R00174